THE CHARITABLE IMPULSE

Wealth and Social Conscience in Communities and Cultures Outside the United States

JAMES A. JOSEPH

The Foundation Center
New York • 1989

Library of Congress Cataloging-in-Publication Data

Joseph, James A. (James Alfred), 1935–
  The charitable impulse : wealth and social conscience in
communities and cultures outside the United States / by James A.
Joseph.
    p.   cm.
  Includes bibliographies and index.
  ISBN 0-87954-300-0 : $24.95. — ISBN 0-87954-301-9 (soft) : $19.95
  1. Philanthropists—Biography. 2. Charities—Cross-cultural
studies. I. Title.
HV27.J67 1989
361.7'092'2—dc20
[B]   89-1412
                                                                      CIP

Dedicated to the memory of my mother, who first sparked my interest in the charitable impulse, to my father, who still preaches about it, and to Doris, Jeffrey, and Denise, who tolerated and even supported my obsession with the subject.

CONTENTS

FOREWORD

JIM JOSEPH, as President of the Council on Foundations, has never been content simply to represent the interests of organized philanthropy in this country; he speaks constantly and universally of its ideals and of its potential as an enobling social force.

In this volume, that vision and voice of leadership emerge again with vibrant clarity. This time Joseph builds on portraiture, sketching the profiles of ten persons of wealth who in cultures other than the U.S. have displayed the charitable impulse, reaching out to help others and to leave the world a better place than what they found.

The ten are in many ways a study in contrasts. They differ not only in origin but also strikingly in charitable mode and motivation. They exhibit a fascinating array of cultural influences, human idiosyncrasies, and often the telltale markings of privilege. Some of the portraits are not in the preferred legendry of altruistic idealism: indulence, self-purification, and questionable sources of wealth lurk alongside other more inspirational models. But Joseph in his collection of illustrative personalities shows himself ready to deal with the warts and blemishes as well as the idealized in his attempt to demonstrate the universality of the charitable impulse.

And in his juxtaposition of the nobler and the not-so-noble, his portraits are the more persuasive: these are recognizable human beings, believable in their variety, convincing in their representation of the diversity as well as the commonality that gives rise to the commitment of private wealth to the public good.

Joseph is clearly and unapologetically an advocate for private philanthropy, and for a globalizing culture that allows room for and builds upon the charitable impulse. He is under no illusion, either that private generosity will automatically be generated or transmitted as a social tradition, or that standing alone, it is sufficient to satisfy the needs of a rapidly complicating society. His chapters on the priority that must be given to cultivating compassion and on the limits of private generosity are powerfully argued.

But one can feel the optimism and idealism from which he writes. The world is rapidly growing to appreciate the social necessity of private philanthropy—not only where it has long flourished but in countries and cultures which have relied primarily on government and central control. Witness the spreading acceptance of private giving and voluntary action in the Soviet Union as but one impressive example.

Seen in the perspective of a globalizing trend, Joseph is as much a prophet as a defender of faith in the essential goodness of individuals.

Paul N. Ylvisaker
Harvard University

PREFACE

THIS BOOK is the product of a life-long interest in how compassionate values are developed, nurtured, and activated. The formal research began while I was in residence at Nuffield College at Oxford University in England and Mishkenot Sha Ananim in Jerusalem, but the moral curiosity, the informal search, began in my father's rural church in the bayou regions of Louisiana. It took me later to the professional study of theology in New England and peaked during my years as an officer of a large business enterprise concerned about what it means to be a responsible corporate citizen in widely different communities and cultures.

I share this personal note to make the point that writing this book has been a labor of love—in some ways the continuation of an inter-generational guest. It is not the work of a psychologist seeking to analyze behavior or of a historian seeking to honor heroes. My professional and academic experiences cover a wide variety of vocations and disciplines, from teaching ethics to professionally dispensing private philanthropy, but my primary interest is in examining why some of the world's wealthy people choose to go beyond normally accepted standards of civic duty and moral obligation while others are obsessed with the private benefits and public privileges of wealth.

Interviews in Caracas, Copenhagen, Tokyo, Jerusalem, and other centers of culture and commerce have had their own special intrigue, but it is the search for the soul of goodness that has consumed me. I have been tempted along the way to restrict this project simply to writing social biography or to analyzing what the classical academic traditions have had to say about altruism and the charitable impulse. Each would have been a good subject for separate books, but in the end I decided that since my own intellectual journey was informed and enriched by both, I could not do justice to the subject unless I brought the insights of both approaches together in one volume. While my major purpose has been to identify the motives and examine the values that lead to acts of generosity, I have also tried to identify personal attributes, human development practices, myths, morality tales, and other vehicles of cultural transmission that bear on my concern with how to maintain a caring society.

Everywhere I have turned, someone has had a favorite benefactor to recommend. This book, however, must necessarily exclude some exceptional contributors to the public good; men and women who did much to mitigate hunger, eliminate disease, improve education, and eradicate all manner of social maladies. It is a book about one of the most noble of human virtues—the charitable impulse—but it is a journey in search of the motives and values that give rise to acts of generosity in societies where there are very few private or public incentives. The concern is with the charitable practices of the wealthy, but the focus is on the motives of the charitable actor rather than the magnitude of the charitable act.

I owe a great deal to all the people who have helped along the way; those who provided information; those who provided access; and those who helped with research, travel arrangements, typing, and all the other activities involved in researching and publishing a work of this sort.

Many of my colleagues in the Hague Club—an organization of executive officers of the larger foundations in Europe and selected representatives from other continents—hosted my visits to their countries and were helpful in arranging interviews in other parts of the world. I am especially grateful to Luisa Pulido and the Mendoza family in Venezuela, Yehuda Elkana and Fred Simon in Israel, James Cornford and Steve Burkeman in England, Willem Welling in Holland,

and Niels and Ulla Petri in Denmark. There were many other very special acts of kindness as well: Rudolf Kerscher of the Fritz Thyssen Stiftung meeting my train in Köln, Germany, with roses for my wife; the Mendoza grandchildren hosting my daughter at the Mendoza farm in Venezuela; and Tadasha Yamamota providing an interpreter in Japan. None of these good people can be held responsible for my conclusions, but they were certainly responsible for my enthusiasm.

This project would never have gotten off the ground had it not been for the able research assistance of Suzanne Nagel and the support and encouragement of Kathleen Selz. Thanks also to Myrtle Mark, Karen Bates, and Karen Lynn. Nothing in this book should be assumed to represent the views of the Council on Foundations. The views expressed are exclusively my own.

James A. Joseph
Washington, D.C.
April 1989

PROLOGUE

The Charitable Impulse

1

Philanthropy at the Crossroads

TALES OF ALTRUISM, CHARITY, AND PHILANTHROPY can be found in every culture and every community, among those with abundant wealth as well as among those who live on the margins of the economy. There are still billionaires living in multimillion-dollar palaces, women with jewel collections that are vast and breathtaking, and oil sultans with harems and an unashamed zest for conspicuous consumption. But for every stereotype there are also exceptions—men and women of means who engage in uncommon acts of generosity. Individual acts of commitment and compassion remain the cornerstone of the benevolent community in many parts of the world, but private philanthropy is in many ways at the crossroads.

There is growing uncertainty, even anxiety, about the continuity of the civic virtues and the resilience of the religious values that lead to private generosity and public benevolence. This uneasiness stems from many factors, but two deserve special attention from those who are interested in maintaining a caring society: 1) much of the new wealth is being created in non-European communities where neither the moral traditions nor the forms of private benevolence are well known to outsiders, and 2) the legacy of private philanthropy so widely celebrated in the United States and Great Britain has appeared in recent years to be endangered by a new money culture that emphasizes fundamentally different values, life-styles, and folk heroes.

Americans, in particular, are just beginning to come to grips with the full implication of the economic and demographic changes that have led to the decline of European dominance abroad and the coming decline in influence of European descendants at home. Now that the vision of a future in which the majority of our citizens will be descendants of non-Europeans has begun to take shape, there is growing interest in the culture, values, attitudes, and social vision of the various groups that constitute the American society. Some Americans are concerned primarily about the impact of these changes on the future work force and the nation's ability to compete in an interdependent world economy. Others are concerned primarily about the impact on educational institutions, how best to deal with cultural pluralism in our colleges, and what cultural adjustments will be required in our schools. But while the impact on educational and economic institutions becomes more and more obvious, very little attention has been given to the implications for politics and philanthropy. No one seems to be asking what these changes portend for the way in which Americans meet social needs and solve social problems. Is there likely to be a greater dependence on government, a greater social role for the public sector, or will the historic pragmatism that has seen us balance private generosity with public benevolence continue?

Recent research has begun to illuminate the benevolent and helping traditions of various minority communities. In addition, increasing numbers of members of these communities have been accumulating wealth. But while they have often been generous in responding to crisis, with the poor often helping the poor, little is known of their view of what constitutes a benevolent community. This, coupled with the marginal status of the many members of these groups who are outside the mainstream economy, has led many Americans to view minority groups as primarily the recipients of charity rather than benevolent communities in their own right.

This is an inaccurate and unfortunate perception. Just as American philanthropy in its first two centuries was a product of the traditions and values of a mixture of immigrant groups largely from Europe, so it will evolve and change in the next century. As the new groups redefine American culture, so are they likely to redefine American philanthropy.

But as this study demonstrates, the concern for neighbor, the forms of benevolence that promote the well-being of others, has no national or cultural boundaries. The charitable impulse is triggered whenever people see themselves as part of a community, whether it be the family, the neighborhood, or the nation. And as the notion of community expands, so does the scope of philanthropy.

The multiculturalism of American philanthropy is not new. The American philanthropic tradition is only fully understood and appreciated when seen as a mosaic of values and traditions that have thrived on American soil, but whose roots are to be found in the religious teachings and civic virtues of very diverse cultures. What is new is the growing recognition that the continuity of social attitudes and institutions will soon be dependent on non-Europeans, whose giving and helping traditions have rarely been acknowledged, studied, or appreciated.

All too few Americans are aware, for example, that in the Asian-American community strong charity/loan systems and family associations, kin networks, and prefixture groups have traditionally been called upon to meet the needs of individual members either for personal or business purposes. Little attention has been paid to the fact that in the African-American community both African family traditions and the American experience of alienation and isolation have fostered collective self-help. Philanthropic activity generally consists as much in the giving of goods, the volunteering of time, and the provision of shelter as in the giving of money, but the benevolence of strong, stable black churches has been dependent on cash gifts as well.

Among Hispanic Americans, giving in many ways mirrors the tradition and practices of the African-American community in that it is almost entirely church-related. Native Americans who established the Seventh Generation Fund, Philippinos, poor blacks, Hispanics, and other groups in the American society who are often thought of as recipients rather than as donors are coming to be seen in a new light. A 1988 survey found that low-income Americans contribute a larger share of their income for charitable purposes than their wealthier colleagues. The survey by the Gallup organization of a representative group of American households showed that among those making charitable contributions, households with incomes below $10,000 gave an average of 2.8 percent of their incomes to charity. Those earning $100,000 or more gave 1.7 percent.

The concentration of many of the non-European groups on the margins or outside the mainstream economy in America has prevented the accumulation of wealth that is a prerequisite to the formation of foundations, charitable trusts, and other mechanisms of organized philanthropy. It is revealing to look at the practices of wealthy people and families in the home countries and cultures from which many of these groups have come. The past charitable practices of the benevolent rich in some countries may have been more of an aberration than normative behavior, but their life stories suggest that the caring impulse that leads to philanthropy has no civic or cultural limits.

A second cause of uncertainty and even anxiety about the future of private benevolence is the resurgence of the Hobbesian idea that human beings are by nature self-centered and uncaring. The 1980s will be remembered as a time in which selfishness, greed, and the pursuit of wealth became the dominant drives of a new money culture that gave respectability and made public virtues of many qualities that were once considered private vices. The decade that began with an almost ritualistic celebration of voluntarism and other-serving values also gave us Ivan Boesky, the Wall Street speculator, who was in many ways the high priest of a new cult fascinated with wealth and power. In the 1980s *Democracy in America* by the French observer Alexis de Tocqueville was one of the most quoted—although probably least read—of our literary legacies. But while some Americans were celebrating the tradition of civic idealism and private benevolence, others were preaching the gospel of self-indulgence, assuring students on college campuses and the young upwardly mobile professionals that greed was not only acceptable but healthy.

Recent attempts to give moral legitimacy to the pursuit of self-interest have not been exclusively American. Shuicho Kato, author of a prize-winning history of Japanese literature, argues that, by and large, "the whole of society is geared to domination and manipulation rather than compassion." Adding that "most people are not very much concerned with other people's suffering," he warns that the attitudes of Japan and much of the rest of the world need to undergo serious change if local and national communities are to live in harmony in an interdependent world.

The view of the English philosopher Thomas Hobbes that human beings are moved chiefly by the desire for power and other selfish considerations is alive in Europe and other parts of the world as well. His idea that human beings are by nature self-centered and uncaring has been given new respectability by social scientists, philosophers, and others who have challenged the notion that altruism is a universal impulse. They argue that me-ism is as much a part of our nature as the will to live. While it has been generally accepted that human nature is more complex than Hobbes supposed, a creed of greed and selfishness still competes for moral legitimacy.

There are those who argue to the contrary, however, that an unprejudiced assessment of human life must reach a different conclusion. To test this assumption, it is only necessary to examine why some people in unlikely places, and under less than encouraging circumstances, have chosen to go beyond normally accepted standards of civic duty and public obligation.

Thus, the ten portraits of benevolent wealth in this volume provide support of three propositions: 1) that while human nature is more complex than Hobbes supposed, if it is possible to identify the factors that give rise to acts of generosity, it may be possible to determine what qualities must be cultivated if we are to remain a caring society; 2) that philanthropy—a form of behavioral altruism—may be more widespread, more widely encouraged, and more formally practiced in the United States than elsewhere, but that the selfless act of giving associated with the Rockefellers, the Vanderbilts, and other wealthy American families can also be found in altogether different cultural and political settings around the world; and 3) that portraits of altruism in action shed more light on the motives for altruistic behavior than Good Samaritan paradigms and theories of moral development.

Altruism, charity, and philanthropy as here examined are by no means synonymous, and while careful definitions can be offered to delineate what is unique about each, portraits set in such widely different political, economic, and moral cultures do not always lend themselves to such careful distinctions. The subjects of these profiles are all people with extensive fortunes, mostly made through the success of competitive business enterprise. They share the fact that they chose to use a large part of their private wealth for public purposes, but their motives and their values are widely different and run the gamut from the most noble to the most self-serving.

Why this concern with motives and values? There is increasing recognition of the need for a body of literature on philanthropy, but it would be a mistake to restrict the efforts to meet this need to simply identifying who gives—how much and for what purposes—or to simply repeating self-serving shibboleths about the uniqueness of the American political system. We may overlook the fact that *why* people give may be as important as *what* they give. Moreover, we may miss the opportunity to encourage and support the development of private voluntary activity and/or charitable sectors in formerly closed societies and communities that are rapidly accumulating new wealth.

The profiles in this volume focus on disparate individuals rather than a distinct cultural typology or national group; on benefactors rather than on beneficiaries; on donors whose resources are substantial, although the world of philanthropy is ennobled and enriched by the humanitarianism, social idealism, and good works of men and women of much less means. This study is a trip into a world of wealth that is intriguing not only because it is foreign to American shores, but because those who made money and chose to use it for public purposes rather than simply private benefits were just as public-spirited as some of the legendary figures in American history.

There are still those who subscribe to the Hobbesian principles, but even the strongest proponent of self-interest theories must ultimately agree that a good society depends as much on the goodness of people as on the soundness of government and the fairness of laws. And so, as men and women around the world consider how best to build and maintain caring communities, there is much to be learned from those who have demonstrated, in some way, a common virtue taught by Moses, Mohammed, Jesus, Buddha, and other great religious leaders: the notion that there is in each of us an urge to connect with another person and to provide solace, comfort, and aid.

In that regard, this book goes beyond social biography to a cross-cultural probe of what qualities must be nurtured and cultivated if we are to remain a caring society. When the profiles are grouped and analyzed for this purpose, it becomes possible to trace the evolution of compassionate values through four stages of consciousness: stage I, in which the spirit of altruism is developed; stage II, in which it is nurtured and reinforced; stage III, in which it is activated; and stage IV, in which the altruist—now a full-scale philanthropist—becomes aware of the limits of private benevolence and the potential of political participation and other forms of private or public sector strategies in achieving desired ends. For most of the wealthy donors, although in very different times and cultures, the charitable impulse grew to include all four stages of consciousness.

The rest of this book examines in detail the development, reinforcement, and activation of the charitable impulse. It begins with a walk through the intricate passageways of behavioral psychology, cultural anthropology, moral theology, socioeconomics, and sociobiology. Subsequent chapters probe even more deeply, but the emphasis is on the individual philanthropist, acknowledging that while academic studies of altruistic impulses are helpful, they are often divorced from the complex web of motives and values that may drive a single act of generosity. Thus, the most telling commentary comes not from the analysis of classical theories, but from the life stories of people who use their private wealth for civic purposes that bring them no financial gain.

One of the final chapters examines what the profiles tell us about how to cultivate the compassionate values that lead to private generosity and public benevolence. The emphasis is on preparing members of the next generation to understand their obligations and to meet their responsibilities to one another.

2

The Soul of Goodness

ALTRUISM CONTINUES to be one of life's mysteries. While the growing body of literature on the subject has given it pride of place in social science research, there is still no consensus on why some people choose to sacrifice their own interest—even their personal wealth—for the good of others. Traditional assumptions have been divided between those who argue that altruistic behavior is a natural impulse and those who consider it to be unnatural and, where found, the result of socialization. Newer disciplines like sociobiology and socioeconomics have brought new theories and variations on old arguments to the arena of debate.

Among the many assumptions regarding the caring impulse, there are three that have special bearing on this probe of the motivations and values that have led wealthy people and families in widely different economic settings to engage in large-scale philanthropy. The first assumption is that there is an altruistic personality, an assumption that leads scholars and researchers to debate whether altruism is a natural human impulse or learned social behavior. The second assumption is that there is a tradition of civic stewardship and *noblesse oblige* in which those favored by wealth are presumed to have an obligation to use some of it for the benefit of the community. The third assumption presupposes a moral imperative—charity as a common virtue taught by the great religious leaders Moses, Mohammed, Jesus, Buddha, and others. These three arguments were the most frequently advanced to explain the motives of the men and women in this study and are, thus, deserving of special attention.

THE ALTRUISTIC PERSONALITY

Research into altruistic behavior has been considerably enlivened by the new—but highly controversial—discipline of sociobiology. In little more than a decade, this new area of scientific inquiry has been responsible for a blossoming of new knowledge of the behavior of animals. While its application to human beings remains hotly contested, this has not stopped researchers from speculating about why people love and why they hate, why they have the urge to reach out to those in need, and why they sometimes seem self-interested and self-serving.

Philanthropy, in the language of sociobiology, derives from and is an extension of, a biological disposition toward altruism. Sociobiologists argue that we are genetically designed to be caring social animals and, therefore, are born and grow up with a natural fondness for each other. We are not only obliged by our genes to be useful to each other, but there is an instinctive urge toward self-sacrifice as well.

Theories of genetic relatedness vary from the argument that the selfish gene is responsible for altruism to the notion of reciprocal altruism. According to the first theory, we would be far more likely to use our private resources for the benefit of those closest to us than those farthest away. Thus we would, for example, be likely to engage in charitable activity that benefits our family, neighborhood, religious community, or other primary relationships. According to the second theory, the charitable act grows out of an expectation of some form of personal gain—whether tangible or intangible.

Those critics who disagree with the idea that altruistic behavior is related to genes point to the apparent "naturalness" of contradictory forms of behavior. They argue that the disposition toward selfishness and *causing* suffering appears to be as natural as the disposition toward self-sacrifice and *eliminating* suffering. Dr. Lewis Thomas, a respected physician and author who has served as dean of the Memorial Sloan-Kettering Cancer Center in New York, is one of a number of scientists who answer that the genetic message is like a distant music and some of us are hard of hearing. According to Thomas, "Societies are noisy affairs, drowning out the sound of ourselves and our connection. Hard of hearing, we go to war. Stone deaf, we make nuclear missiles. Nonetheless, the music is there, waiting for more listeners."

The idea that altruism is genetically determined is rejected with as much fervor as it is advanced. *Sociobiology,* the encyclopedic book by Harvard entomologist Edward O. Wilson, which first drew public attention to the assertions of sociobiologists, has given rise to a number of highly critical evaluations of this maturing field of study. But the greatest contribution of sociobiology may have been its success in causing scholars in other disciplines to look anew at the soul of goodness.

The study of altruism in behavioral psychology is a good example. For some time psychologists, in particular, have been on the cutting edge of research into why people reach out to each other. Erik Erikson was advancing a long-held view when, in his definitive work on the subject published in 1969, he attributed Mohandas Gandhi's altruism to an effort to expiate unconscious guilt. In *Gandhi's Truth on the Origins of Militant Nonviolence,* Erikson sought to explain altruism as the reinforcement people get from making themselves feel good by doing good. Behavior geneticists have not been willing to go as far as their colleagues in sociobiology, but many have sought to determine whether there is an inherent temperament that predisposes some people toward acts of kindness.

When the clinical psychologist Abraham Maslow sought to assess the qualities of mature, fufilled people, he characterized them as displaying a sense of obligation, affection, sympathy, and social responsibility. His theory of a "needs hierarchy" introduced in the July 1942 issue of *Psychologic Review* in an article entitled "A Theory of Human Motivation" has led others to go even further, pointing to the need for human beings to "relate," "belong," and "to love each other" as essential conditions of community and personal fulfillment.

Yet, two of the major figures in psychology, Sigmund Freud and Erich Fromm, have reached fundamentally different conclusions about altruistic behavior. In *Civilization and its Discontents*, first published in 1830 in German, Freud portrays man as an essentially aggressive individual who strives for gratification, but who is kept under control by the forces of civilization. Here Freud, the psychologist, is essentially agreeing with Thomas Hobbes, the philosopher. Erich Fromm, on the other hand, disagreed with both Freud's and Hobbes' view of human nature, concluding that the capacity for affection and generosity is part of what it means to be a mature, healthy individual.

Sigmund Freud and Erich Fromm have been the major theorists in the field, but useful insights also come from newer researchers like Dr. Samuel Oliner, who at the age of twelve slipped away from the gestapo in a Polish village. He has long been engaged in an effort to understand why non-Jews were willing to risk their lives to help Jews avoid the death chambers of the Nazis. The findings from his Altruistic Personality Project have great implications for understanding the charitable impulse as well.[1] Like a variety of other studies, Dr. Oliner's results point to the formative experiences people have in childhood, which seem to make them reach out to others in need.

Oliner has identified three specific elements that he believes combine to lead individuals to acts of compassion. The first is compassionate values. He and others, like Perry London, a Harvard psychologist, point to a parent or some other person who was strong on moral values as having influenced the altruist at an early age. The second element Oliner has identified is a sense of competence, a strong belief by the actor that he/she was capable of succeeding in the act. The third element was the wherewithal to put the sense of values and competence to the real test— to engage in the altruistic act. In the case of the rescuers, this involved a particular expertise, but also a willingness to take risks.

Ervin Staub, a psychologist at the University of Massachusetts and author of the two-volume work *Positive Social Behavior and Morality*, went one step further than Oliner, suggesting in 1978 that altruism also needs proximity, a close enough involvement in the need to transform the self-image in the process. According to Staub, the altruist isn't born; he/she evolves. The individual may begin with only a small commitment, but once that first step is taken, he/she begins to see himself/ herself differently, as not simply one who is capable of helping, but as one who helps. When what starts out as a mere will becomes an act, it is more likely to become a continuing involvement.

While evolutionary biologists give priority to inborn impulses, and behavioral psychologists concentrate on habit formation, economists see human actions as guided by rational intelligence. Man as *Homo economicus* is out to maximize his self-interest. This thesis was at the heart of the argument that won the 1986 Nobel Prize in Economic Sciences for James Buchanan. The George Mason University professor argued that our politicians, acting like the rest of us, put the maximization of their own interests and those of their special-interest clients ahead of the general welfare. The father of what is called "public choice theory," Buchanan published *Liberty, Market, and State* in 1985 and *The Political Economy of Budget Deficits* in 1986, in which he argued that to bring significant changes in government spending or taxation, a policy initiative must involve a fundamental shift in incentives.

The Buchanan emphasis on self-interest is countered by the newer discipline of socioeconomics spearheaded by Amitai Etzioni, who teaches at George Washington University—just a few miles up the road from where Buchanan is applying the analytical tools and teachings of classical economics to the arena of politics. Etzioni argued in a January 1987 article in *The Washington Post* on "Socio-Economics" that people have dual personalities. They are indeed part debased—drawn by quests for pleasure and self-interest. But they are also part noble—seeking to serve humane purposes and to act morally.

Socioeconomics is a young upstart compared to classical economics, but its adherents argue that they are not only out to change the dismal claims of their discipline but also to relate it to what they know about values. They argue that while people may set out to maximize their interest, they purposefully limit themselves, because their emotions and values tell them that some options are unthinkable and that others serve larger purposes.

COMMITMENT TO COMMUNITY

Homo economicus is also *Homo communalis*. Economic man is also man in community. The studies of altruism as an individual act have their parallels in studies of the behavior of social groups. Anthropologists who have studied the concept of giving in archaic societies have generally confirmed the degree to which individuals were enmeshed in a complex pattern of mutual rights and obligations and how gift exchanges promoted social cohesion. The most important such study may be the work of Marcel Mauss, who described the charitable impulse as the result, on the one hand, of a moral idea about gifts and wealth and, on the other, of an idea about sacrifice.[2] His studies of early societies in ancient Rome and Melanesia demonstrate that the practice of giving was grounded in moral, religious, mythological, and social phenomena quite similar to the social conventions and impulses of modern society.

Benevolence in early communities was expressed through an extensive family or clan system in which the boundaries of the community were defined by blood relationships. Mutual obligations were assumed in such communities, but the bond was cemented by the giving of gifts. If the major benefactor was a hereditary chief who provided food and protection, the beneficiaries responded with gifts to the provider. But there were many other elaborate and sometimes ceremonial practices of gift exchange as well. They often included the welcoming of a guest, the treatment of the bereaved during periods of mourning, or the honoring of youth or age. Giving was not only an important expression of "other-serving" values, the act of giving was often a moment of high drama or cultural ritual in which the cultural meaning and self-understanding of the giver, the receiver, and the community were affirmed.

In simple societies, kinship predominated as a means of creating community, but as societies became more complex, kinship became more ambiguous and less significant. Robert Bellah and his associates in *Habits of the Heart* remind us that friendship has also been a key element in creating social solidarity and social obligation. According to Bellah, friendship and its virtues are not merely private: they are public, even political, for a civic order, a city, is above all a network of friends.[3] While Bellah's observations are historically accurate, others like Parker Palmer speak of the present-day community as a company of strangers. People meet and act together in their common interest without ever becoming friends.[4]

The idea of friendship as a basis for communal identity and social obligations was first introduced by Aristotle, elaborated by Cicero, and understood for centuries as a sentiment that creates social solidarity.

This classical concept of friendship has three essential components: friends enjoy each other's company, they are useful to each other, and they share a commitment to a common good.[5]

It was the third component, shared commitment to a common good, that led to many private benefactions for the benefit of the community. But as the historian Joel T. Rosenthal points out in *The Purchase of Paradise*, many of the benefactors in the Middle Ages were responding as much to societal expectations as to private notions of civic obligation. All men of property were expected to give to the Church and to the poor, during life and at death.[6] Rosenthal accused them not only of seeking to justify their inequitable status in the social hierarchy, but also of attempting to buy prayers for their own souls as well.[7] Thus, he described the ultimate motive for much of the benevolent wealth of that time as the purchase of paradise.

The medieval practice of alms-giving also gave rise to the concept of *noblesse oblige*. In Europe it represented the duties attendant upon noble birth, but in other countries devoid of hereditary aristocracy it took on a different meaning. It was simply interpreted as the duty of the rich to the society that had enriched them—the notion that successful citizens owe a dual obligation of time and money to the communities in which they prospered.

Closely allied with the tradition of *noblesse oblige* was the code of the gentleman. Whereas nobility was guided by the myths, mystique, legends, and practices of the land baron, the gentleman was concerned with etiquette. He not only prided himself on good manners, honor, and bravery, but he also took delight in acts of generosity. The prototype of the gentleman was the English squire, whose people—tenants, family, and neighbors—were his personal responsibility. While each society developed its own version, the code of the gentleman always included the idea of civic responsibility. He appealed to tradition and etiquette, and prided himself on his public services to his constituents and his community, but his benefactions were often rooted in the need to see himself as a charitable being, a good person. Like the proprietor of the orphanage in Charles Dickens' *Oliver Twist*, or the horrid stepfamily to which Jane Eyre was indentured, the squire attended to the poor more for public approbation than from an innate altruism or a moral desire to do good.

The tradition of benevolent wealth also has roots in the notion of stewardship, the idea that the resources of the earth—whether wealth or talent—are held in trust for a divine purpose and through the intervention of divine power. The central claim of the stewardship tradition is that our relationship to land or financial resources may be by law or custom defined as ownership, but in the deepest and most fundamental sense it is a conditional form of trusteeship. We are stakeholders in a civic enterprise where self and society share not only common opportunities but common obligations. In the true sense of the old English word "steward," we are responsible for prudent management of an estate that is not our own.

THE MORAL IMPERATIVES OF RELIGION

The evolution of this idea of stewardship can be traced from the earliest forms of religion to the religious teachings of the Twentieth Century. The idea that of all the virtues to be made part of each of us, the greatest is charity, comes from Moses as well as Mohammed; Jesus as well as Budhha. It comes from the Koran, the Torah, and the Bible. Even Confucius argued that "goodness is God," and that while God may not necessarily be a Supreme Being apart from us, He is at least a supreme state of being within us. Charity in its Latin form, *caritas*, first meant "dearness," as in the affectionate relations between members of a family. But it also came to refer to the compassion of an individual for those outside his own family as well. The focus was on the individual in need; the hungry and the sick as well as those who render aid to someone in trouble. The Good Samaritan was the prototype of the charitable impulse in the early Christian Church. The moral imperative was love.

The Jewish tradition of charity also included the selfless act, but it was undergirded by a concern for the oppressed. The moral imperative was justice. The object of the giving was not simply the relief of suffering but its ultimate elimination.

In Islam, benevolence was formalized into one of the five obligatory virtues or "pillars" of religious faith. This concept of charity originated in the early days of Islam from the simple belief that worldly possessions obfuscated the true purity of life. So the Muslim was expected to practice the virtues of benevolence and justice in order to retain a relative state of purity.

The concept of *tsedakah*, which is interchangeable with modern English usages of the words "righteousness" and "charity," dominates both the moral tradition and the public policies pursued by the Jewish community. As Jacob Neusner put it in a 1985 article in *Foundation News* magazine, "The Jew does not give simply because he feels like it, but because it is his obligation." Many of the earliest concepts of charity in the Jewish tradition were later organized into formal codes and laws. According to Neusner, the Jewish law makes one fundamental point: "The poor person must enjoy self-respect and dignity." What Judaism requires, therefore, is consideration for the humanity of the recipient, who remains no different from the donor. Those who receive are not less than or different from those who give. They have not only need, but also feelings. They welcome not only our beneficence but also our respect. So when we engage in the act of giving we must do so in such a way that the equality of the giver and the receiver is acknowledged. This is not an act of grace or even an expression of affection. It is, for the faithful Jew, an act of respect, an expression of duty.[8]

Neusner, who is University Professor and distinguished scholar of Judaic Studies at Brown University, argues that we therefore notice two things. First, it is not necessary for the donor to know who gets, or for the recipient to know who gives. Second, the situation of the donor is as important as that of the recipient. It is not enough to give. Giving must be done with thought. It must be marked by reflection, respect for the other party, and enhanced humility on the part of the donor. Accordingly, the bottom line is this: *how* you give matters at least as much as *what* you give; this is the meaning of the Jewish laws of *tsedakah*. As Neusner summarizes it, "We Jews move from what is required of us to what we are required to become."

The contributions of Christianity to the understanding of the charitable impulse are manifold. The early Christians were among the first to acknowledge that virtue alone would not feed the poor. Thus, from the beginning, moral precepts were joined with behavioral injunctions. A vocabulary of duty and obligation developed alongside the language of reward and punishment. Just as for the Jew, for whom the concepts of righteousness and charity were fused into the term *tsedakah*, for the Christian the concept of *agape* came to represent a coalescence of love and charity. And it is this notion of love that forms the basis of all moral life. *Agape* is not the same as liking, but it involves an unconditional acceptance. The neighbor who is to be loved is anybody.

Those who analyze the moral imperatives of *agape* usually describe at least two clusters of obligation. First, because we recognize one another as part of a common humanity, we admit "negative duties" not to kill, enslave, or cause social injury to others. Second, we accept "positive duties" to provide unselfish, direct assistance to anyone who is suffering or in dire need. This principle is sometimes called "Samaritanism," that is, it is associated with the New Testament story of the Good Samaritan, the traveler who stopped to give aid and comfort to an injured stranger.

Samaritanism creates an obligation to help those in need. It may even involve self-sacrifice. But more importantly, it is a moral imperative rather than a casual or voluntary act. Generosity, like mercy, patience, and kindness, is a virtue that flows from the human will, but it is conditioned by religious covenant and divine command.

H. Richard Niebuhr, one of the Twentieth Century's great theologians, spent a lifetime probing the roots and fundamental character of the moral life. No one who ever studied under him or engaged him in the discussion of Christian ethics can ever forget his preoccupation with the concept of responsibility, the understanding of the self as social, living in "response-relations" to other selves. The key to the moral life was for him both the freedom and flexibility of "responsiveness" to others and the guiding ideal of "responsibility" to, and for, the community.

Reinhold Niebuhr, who worked out a theology that sought to retain the Reformation values of Martin Luther while applying them to present-day social problems, also emphasized the social nature and moral responsibilities of the individual. But he was more concerned than his brother Richard with the paradox of the obvious universal humanity and the "tribal loyalties" that limit and restrict the sense of obligation among human beings. The tribal limits (race, culture, nationality, language, and even religion) of our sense of responsibility remained for him the chief source of our inhumanity to one another. In *Man's Nature and His Communities,* Niebuhr wrote that any distinguishing mark between the "we group," in which mutual responsibilities are acknowledged, and a "they group," who are presumed to be beyond the pale of our humanity, serves the tribal character of human nature.[9] What saves the self from destructive tribal limits and undue self-regard is the primacy of grace and transcendence. The notion of the self is tied to a larger system of loyalty and meaning, thus creating both a strong sense of interconnectedness, and moral obligation to the community.

For the Christian, then, philanthropy in its most ideal state does not seek reciprocity or mutuality. It is self-giving without being self-serving, and it goes beyond tribal limits to embrace all of the created order.

The various claims of theology, psychology, economics, anthropology, and biology can be argued and analyzed forever, but when all the theories have been examined, one is still left with the question that has been debated for centuries: Is private benevolence the product of a natural impulse or learned social behavior? There are no simple answers. If there were, the debate would have been long settled. The portraits of benevolent wealth in the following pages seek to illuminate the arguments by giving flesh and blood to what have been essentially abstract theories and theologies.

What stands out in many of the profiles is that in order to act in such a way that others are the primary beneficiaries, there must be an element of self-denial. However, to act altruistically—to engage in acts of generosity—is not necessarily to act contrary to one's self-interest. Even the most honored and noble benefactions often involve some form of congruence between the welfare of others and the interest of the self or a "primary" community. But this form of enlightened self-interest should not be confused with the more narrow selfish interest. Enlightened self-interest focuses primarily on the benefit for others—although some form of satisfaction may accrue to the benefactor, while selfish interest begins and ends with the expected benefit or utility to the donor.

The profiles that follow have been grouped together according to the dominant passions that appear to have inspired individuals from very different backgrounds to acts of generosity. They include the religious

PART ONE

Wealth and Civic Duty

INTRODUCTION

Wealth and
Civic Duty

THE NOTION OF SOCIALLY RESPONSIBLE WEALTH first flourished in England and later reached new levels in the United States. But it would be a mistake to assume that the idea of civic duty has had national or cultural boundaries. In England, the tradition became so established that the failure of the wealthy to donate some substantial and conspicuous charitable trust or gift was generally regarded as little short of shocking, unless there had been some grievous wasting of the estate because of age, ill-health, or commercial misfortune.[1]

In a study of charity and cultural perspectives in early Chicago, Kathleen McCarthy observed that the rich, by virtue of their leisure, breeding, education, and success were deemed ideally suited to minister to the needs of the city.[2] But there also developed a tradition of civic idealism in which men and women of means in many other countries used their private wealth to support nation-building, the elimination of poverty and disease, and even the establishment of justice. They went beyond the early English notion of charity to develop the modern idea of philanthropy.

A new industrial elite—hard-nosed but benevolent capitalists—emerged in the late Nineteenth and early Twentieth Centuries. Set in widely different cultures and with few obvious similarities except success in business, they began to parcel out their fortunes in a voluntary redistribution of their wealth. The new group of socially conscious industrialists included Lord Nuffield in England; Calouste Gulbenkian, the Armenian of Turkish descent who made and distributed a fortune in support of Armenian communities throughout the world and for the acquisition of valuable pieces of art; Jamsetji Tata in India, whose family was later described as the "Rockefellers of Asia"; and Eugenio Mendoza in Venezuela who helped to set up 5 percent giving clubs among the business corporations in Caracas long before the movement caught on in the United States.

This first phase of benevolent wealth among the new industrial elite was not completely disinterested philanthropy, but a form of "welfare capitalism." It was what has come to be described as *enlightened self-interest*. Most of the industrialists started out with corporate practices that were beyond the acknowledged and accepted obligations of an employer for his employees and their communities. Some were motivated by an explicit desire to achieve a private sector alternative to socialism. Others simply wanted to repay society for their good fortune. But they were all convinced that a satisfied, well-paid, well-fed, well-housed, and healthy worker was more likely to be productive. So they committed a portion of their profits to doing good because they believed it would better enable their companies to do well.

While this small but growing band of disparate entrepreneurs was responding similarly to common commitments and concerns, they were not acting out of a common body of thought or experience. Some knew, or knew about, each other, but welfare capitalism at its formative stage was an uncoordinated set of managerial responses to the needs of a particular community or country. The welfare capitalism practiced by this new class of benevolent industrialists was eventually transformed into a more personalized and professionalized form of philanthropy. They sought to use their personal wealth for the benefit of the community in much the same way that they used corporate profits to provide extended benefits for their workers. Many were nationalists motivated by a desire to contribute to the economic advancement of their national communities. Others believed they had an obligation to use a portion of their wealth to improve the lot of their fellow citizens. But all of them shared the sense of civic duty reflected in the life stories of the three philanthropists profiled in Part One. Each represented, in his own time and place, what we have come to describe as the tradition of civic stewardship.

3

Eugenio Mendoza
Venezuela

OVERLOOKING THE CITY OF CARACAS on the mountainside campus of the Universidad Metropolitana is a statue of the Venezuelan industrialist Eugenio Mendoza. This monument to South America's premier philanthropist seems both at home and out of place in its tranquil academic setting; at home because Mendoza loved the mountains and enjoyed this view of his beloved city of red roofs; out of place because he was a man of action seemingly more at home with doers than with thinkers.

Theodore Levitt, a Harvard marketing professor, makes a distinction between creativity, which is "thinking up new things," and innovation, which is "doing new things." Don Mendoza's family and friends describe him as a man who was always doing new things, willing to risk failure—whether in business or in philanthropy—but succeeding in both because he understood that the process of learning what works includes learning what doesn't work. He had a strong commitment to excellence and surrounded himself with the best minds available; but his genius was his ability to lean on intuition rather than simply logic.

Mendoza's wealth was prodigious. His business acumen led to the establishment of dozens of companies—ranging from a cement group with its own shipping fleet to paper, chemical, financial, and animal feed enterprises that now serve worldwide markets. Motivated by a strong sense of nationalism, he redefined the relationship between rich and poor. He used his wealth to introduce new social benefits for his workers, to improve the quality of life within their communities, and to build a stronger country.

Venezuela seems like an improbable place for a philosophy of wealth that emphasized the social responsibility of the rich—the belief that every man has an obligation to help his fellow man as soon as he has the opportunity to do so. This tropical nation, graced with the inviting beaches of the Caribbean Sea, enjoys a yearly temperature in the 80s. It would seem to be the perfect setting for the stereotype of the idle Latin American rich, blind to the poverty around them.

Yet, it was here that Mendoza introduced bonuses and profit-sharing for his workers and plunged energetically into community development, building thousands of homes for the poor, who lived in tin-and-board "ranchos." Here, too, he established the first foundation in Venezuela, and organized 2 to 5 percent giving clubs within the local business community long before the idea caught on in the United States.

Eugenio Mendoza (1906–1979) once described his life as an extension of his father's: "He was always full of ideas for a better Venezeula. I wanted to be like him but to have the means to make his dreams come true." The elder Mendoza traced his ancestry to Venezeula's first president. On Eugenio's mother's side, the family lineage went back to the South American liberator Simón Bolívar, who was born in Caracas in 1783. But the seven children grew up in modest circumstances, inheriting not wealth but a deep sense of social responsibility. Although Simón Bolívar is now revered throughout Venezuela—the monetary unit is called a bolivar and buildings, streets, and plazas bear his name—his descendants maintained a sense of humility about their heritage.

Eugenio Mendoza grew up in the nine-mile valley where the forested mountain, Mt. Avila, separates Caracas from the sea. He mixed easily and happily among a conservative Catholic population that generally emulated the European elite. Yet, compared to other South American countries, Venezuela (Caracas in particular) was relatively progressive. Banned at the end of the Nineteenth Century, the Roman Catholic church's hold on Venezuela loosened, creating a less structured family life and a secularism that still exists. Eduardo Mendoza, Eugenio's younger brother, fondly recalls, however, that their parents taught values through example. "Conversation between old and young people in a family is now lost, but we had it in our family. During dinner and afterwards, there was usually a strong conversation about our country—creating a strong sense of responsibility." Eduardo described his father as a dreamer, always optimistic about the future of Venezuela. "We needed optimism to survive the difficult conditions of the time." But the elder Mendoza was also a man of action; a strong conservationist, he gathered his children on weekends to plant seedlings on Mt. Avila.

Eugenio Mendoza's mother was a strong personality in her own right. Despite the pervasiveness of the macho tradition in the Venezuelan personality, she aggressively contributed to the spirit of voluntarism that penetrated her household, serving for a time as president of the Venezuelan Red Cross. According to Eduardo, she was a "strong, demanding, but friendly person who took care of everything with tremendous detail and pleasure. She used to sing with happiness even when working." Like her husband, she had a great admiration for the "heroes and builders" of Venezuela. Her optimism was infectious.

While most of the Mendoza children went on to higher education and professional careers, Eugenio ended his formal schooling at the age of seventeen, when he dropped out to take a job as an office boy. In three years, he had become a working partner. After six years, he was the owner, personally delivering barrels of cement, bricks, and roofing supplies with a horse and cart. The charitable impulse that had addicted the Mendoza family even in modest circumstances quickly took on a special character for Eugenio, the entrepreneur. He split 30 percent of his profits with his delivery man and two clerks. The notion of profit-sharing was born. Mendoza employees responded with an enthusiasm and productivity that led to new profits and new ventures. Their youthful boss turned more and more to his father's dreams of a better Venezuela, reviving the country's limping cattle industry and creating a poultry industry; expanding the cement business and providing jobs in badly neglected rural areas. But as his business interests grew, so did his concern for his employees. Profit-sharing was not enough. Too many Mendoza workers seemed unable to translate their growing prosperity into an improved quality of life.

A visit to the cement plant in Pertigilete, an area once infested with malaria-breeding swamps and crippled by alarming illiteracy rates, gives flesh and blood to the humanity of the Mendoza business philosophy. Social workers circulate among employees. The company's medical clinic takes care of the needs of both workers and their families. A company-built and operated school provides educational opportunities for employee children at the plant site while another company-built school serves the community. A company-sponsored program helps to provide housing, and the company social workers make home visits to help employee spouses set up family budgets and deal with other family necessities. Ask a Mendoza employee if this is paternalism, and you are likely to hear a lecture on the social conscience of Eugenio Mendoza, the entrepreneur who believed that whenever profits were reinvested into the company, a comparable amount should go to provide additional social benefits for workers.

Carla Ravell, a former Venezuelan government worker and United Nations official, set up the company's Social Work Department. Ravell speaks with a special passion about her former boss. "He was very much loved by those working for him, by all Venezuelans," she proclaimed in an office interview at the orthopedic hospital Mendoza set up to provide free treatment for polio victims. Ravell cited an example of the affection for Don Eugenio. "When I took a taxi and the driver asked me where I worked, he would say I was very lucky. 'Eugenio Mendoza is a great man. I wished I worked for him. If I did I would have a house. My family would be in a house.' This was the reputation he had—the man who believed that every employee should have a house. About 80 percent of the Mendoza workers in 1978 had their own homes."

Carla Ravell spoke not only with passion but with a penetrating philosophical insight into the man she had known for fifty years. "He was the new ideologist of a new managerial doctrine." When reminded that others spoke of his simple, direct, nonideological style, she answered, "I call him that because he was a man who understood the sociability of money. For him, money was important, money could create power, but it should be used to fulfill a social responsibility to your employees, your community, your country."

Mendoza's social conscience led first to a personal commitment to the well-being of his workers and then to a highly successful campaign to enlist his fellow entrepreneurs in a collaborative effort to stamp out human misery in Venezuela. The April 1963 issue of *Time* magazine quotes him as saying, "We businessmen always talk about the need to make dividends for our shareholders, but we must also create a dividend for the community."

These were not empty words. In the same year that the *Time* article appeared in the United States, Mendoza was one of 100 Venezuelan executives who met to discuss the theme "Corporate Responsibility in Social Progress." This conference, which met for several days in the town of Maracay, was the beginning of what became the "dividendo" movement. Mendoza urged his colleagues to join him in "the development of a far-reaching, coordinated social action program, to be financed by contributions from business firms based on a percentage of annual profits, with the object of reinforcing existing projects and agencies and of stimulating the creation of new ones."

The Maracay convention stimulated the incorporation of the Dividendo Voluntario para la Communidad. Commonly known as "Dividendo," the organization institutionalized the ideals of Don Eugenio into a formal creed. The 130 businessmen who signed the initial charter declared that the higher purposes of private enterprise are "to serve society and to contribute to the creation of socio-economic conditions which promote the integral development of man and the welfare of the community." Making it clear that they referred to more than what has come to be known as "the bottom line," the Dividendo declaration went on to say that "private enterprise must meet a series of social obligations and responsibilities." Therefore, it is necessary that "it assign a percentage of its benefits to improve human capital" and engage in "a permanent effort to enhance the common good." Within three years, Dividendo had 500 corporate members, each pledging to contribute from 2 to 5 percent of corporate net earnings.

But as the oil boom burst on Venezuela, sparking new wealth, a new selfishness emerged. Sitting in his office in a prototypical Spanish hacienda, Julio Sosa Rodriguez, the Venezuelan Ambassador to the United States from 1969 to 1972, lamented the way in which oil riches "distorted the true way of being of the average Venezuelan. We have all these new characters who fly around in jets, but that's not the true Venezuela." Describing Eugenio Mendoza as "a true Venezuelan," he remembered him as a man "who made a fortune—who was highly regarded—but never changed from being a simple man. He was the kind of individual who was just as at ease talking to the president of the Republic as he would be walking out my front door and talking to a guy cleaning my car." Recalling his stint in the United States and travels abroad, he went on to say, "I have met many people in my time, but none like that."

So why did Mendoza swim against the tide, profiting from the oil boom but using it to increase his philanthropy rather than engage in conspicuous consumption? To invest in the future of Venezuela while the newly rich were investing outside the country, causing Caracas to become known as the "capital of capital flight"? The answer was easy for Ambassador Rodriguez: Mendoza was "devoted to his country. He was not a chauvinist but a staunch nationalist. He believed in the future of the country—that people were good." According to Rodriguez, Mendoza's philanthropy grew out of his sense of history. "His family went back to the days before independence. With that kind of history, you develop a sense of belonging, a sense of community." The new selfishness remained a matter of concern. "There are a lot of selfish people in the world and I think we have our share in our country. But if a person is committed to a country and expects it to be the place for the next generation—as it was for the last—there is a special commitment to the future."

Julio Sosa Rodriguez first met Eugenio Mendoza when he was a little boy. Their families had been friends for generations, but they met in Paris when Eugenio was twenty-five years old and Julio eight. Julio was also related to Luisa Mendoza, Eugenio's wife, whom he described as "a cultured lady who provided an elegant household in which to bring up children." Ambassador Rodriguez seemed like the right person to ask about the values that shaped the Mendoza social conscience. He not only knew Mendoza well, but they once shared a ranch together, and in the early days they often spent a day and a half traveling to get there. As Rodriguez put it, "When you spend quite a few days together in different circumstances you get to know a person, and I would say he was a religious man—not the kind of person always in and out of church or praying publicly, but he was related to the Supreme Being in the sense that he understood the commandment to love your neighbor as yourself." Reminded that others saw no particular religious motives behind the Mendoza philanthropy, he suggested that it was difficult for him, as a very religious man, not to think that Eugenio Mendoza had "an inner inspiration that went beyond social feeling."

Armando Espinoza, who began as a secretary to Mendoza and rose to become head of the cement group and the number-two man in the Mendoza enterprises, saw the Mendoza philanthropy as part of Eugenio's innate conception of work. "Since he started to work in 1926," said Espinoza, "he felt the responsibility inherent in the profits of work; in the concept of work itself. . . . I do not know what values or influences moved him. I believe it was spontaneous, part of his nature, of his way of being himself."

Venezuelans are unanimous in their sense that Mendoza was his own man, marching to his own drummer. But there were influences in his life besides Simón Bolívar, his father, and even his sense of destiny. It is more than a coincidence that the library at the university Mendoza established is dedicated to Pedro Grases, the Latin American humanist who taught at Harvard in the 1940s and was one of Mendoza's closest confidants. Professor Grases came to Venezuela in the 1930s as an immigrant from Barcelona, Spain. He first came to know Eugenio's older brother, Carlos, but soon he and Eugenio became close friends.

According to Manuel Acedo Mendoza, Eugenio's nephew, Professor Grases for many years gave his uncle lessons in grammar, writing, history, and culture in general. Acknowledging that this was not generally known, he confessed pride in disclosing it because it said a lot about Eugenio the man. "It was a kind of secret between him and Professor Grases, who also made recommendations of books to read." That is probably what Manuel Acedo's uncle, Eduardo, had in mind when he described Eugenio as "self-made from all points of view—in culture as well as work, taking private lessons in English and history." To Professor Grases, Mendoza was the "premier citizen of the Twentieth Century," a rich man who remained a model citizen, a man of vision "who saw the immediate future and anticipated exactly what has occurred. Every Mendoza enterprise was an anticipation of the needs of the country in the future." In his library at his home, Grases remembered Mendoza as a "self-made man who continued to grow until his death, a passionate man uniquely able to motivate others."

Another important Mendoza influence was his wife, Luisa. Together, they created the Fundación Eugenio Mendoza to lend aid and assistance to the children and youth of Venezuela, to organize and contribute to cultural works, and to promote the creation of entities dedicated to scientific and experimental research. But Luisa was more than Eugenio's handmaiden in philanthropy and mother of four children. Educated in France, she is described by all who know her as a sophisticated, cultivated lady. Her father was Ambassador to England, and she left Venezuela when she was one year old, returning when she was twenty-one. As her daughter Gertrudis observed, "She had a very different upbringing from my father. They made a good combination. Daddy's mentality was that he had to work. Mommy helped him to focus on other things, paintings, etc." Put another way by her cousin Julio Sosa Rodriguez, "Luisa Mendoza was a lady in every sense of the word. She gave Eugenio a lot of polish in dealing with people from other parts of the world."

A very modest and attractive woman, Luisa Mendoza took special delight in talking about her husband, showing off his favorite medals and describing him as a frustrated architect as she entertained at the home they shared together. She considers her husband's greatest accomplishment to be "the eradication of poliomyelitis through the work done in the Foundation Against Children's Paralysis (which later became the Orthopedic Hospital)." Among his many contributions, however, he personally came to regard the Metropolitan University Foundation as his most significant, since it was geared toward training students in the fields required for development. According to Luisa

Mendoza, Eugenio felt the desire to help people at an early age; however, his charitable work consolidated for the first time when he was thirty-six years old. "At that time he was deeply moved by the illness and death of the daughter of a good friend who had suffered from poliomyelitis, a disease rarely treated in Venezuela at the time." It was, therefore, "as an answer to the lack of medical facilities for such cases in children that he created the Orthopedic Hospital. From then on he expanded his charitable work and created a vast array of foundations and institutions." His peers viewed him as a pacesetter, a demanding leader whose goals represented a realistic vision of a new era. His employees and the public knew him as a man who had advanced ideas, but his wife Luisa remembers him as "a man who was never dull." All of the members of the family—including the grandchildren—tell stories of his early rising, his love for polo, and his fascination with Mt. Avila. He was a man with "lots of energy," but a remarkable discipline as well. His associates in the Mendoza enterprises remember his ability to take ten-minute naps, awakening himself with no outside help at exactly the appointed time.

Mendoza's friendship with Nelson Rockefeller may have influenced his decision to use the private foundation model for much of his philanthropy. He consulted Rockefeller regarding some of his charitable activities, and he borrowed ideas from the American foundations and institutions he visited. But he transformed these ideas into philanthropic activities unique to the Venezuelan political and cultural context. His views of the social role of government are not generally known, but he served two brief stints in government, first as a cabinet minister and later as a member of a ruling junta. On each occasion, he resigned after a very brief tenure. Julio Rodriguez surmised that Mendoza went into government because he was asked, but he was impatient with the way in which government functions—the meetings, the campaigns, the slowness of the bureaucracy. "It becomes somewhat frustrating when you are accustomed to doing things and getting results pretty fast," Rodriquez observed. "It is difficult to adapt yourself to political life where it is true you may influence a broader spectrum of issues but the results are sometimes much slower in coming."

Eugenio Mendoza may have been impatient with the political process, but his wife Luisa described the presidential medal as his favorite. It was awarded to him in 1958, when he served as co-president of the Venezuelan junta.

Mendoza was not a professional politician, but he could not escape the politics of his time. In the 1960s, when communist groups began to flex their muscle in South America, they singled him out as a symbol of the hated capitalist. Not only was he the most distinguished businessman in Venezuela, but he had a public image of a generous man, one who had made capitalism humane. So the communist groups took aim at his image, seeking to discredit businessmen as a class. His face appeared on their literature. His name was denounced through graffiti on residential and commercial walls throughout the city of Caracas. Mendoza was both hurt and concerned. He decided to respond, to put his case to the people, to explain to them who he was and what his enterprise did. Among other things, a book was written and employee meetings were held.

It was at such a meeting in 1964 that Mendoza met Clementine Gomez, who came to play a major role in implementing the Mendoza social philosophy. As Gomez recalled in her office at the Metropolitan University, "I was young, twenty-five, at the time, but in this meeting I asked to say a few words. I said what I thought. . . . We didn't need detailed information about the Mendoza Group or the foundations because we believed in what he was doing." Mendoza sought Gomez out after the meeting, and she started working for him directly. She did interviews around the country and concluded that "it was difficult to diminish the Mendoza image." After a year, the attacks against Mendoza ceased, but Gomez remained on the payroll and eventually became head of the company's Department of Human Resources.

Describing herself as a person who was straightforward, Gomez saw one of her roles as "telling Mr. Mendoza the truth." He needed people "who believed in his work but were not afraid to offer criticism." She went on to say, "To talk about Mr. Mendoza is to talk about things being done. He didn't talk about doing, he did." But even more important, "He made it possible for others to do things." He was the kind of leader who used his power to activate power in others.

Mendoza made it possible for his workers to advance their economic and social well-being, seeking 100 percent literacy and offering a bonus to each employee who mastered reading and writing, providing on-the-job training, subsidizing employee lunches and life insurance, and putting as much as 40 percent of his company's profits into year-end wage bonuses. He made it possible to eliminate the two major threats to public health, supporting the work of Dr. Arnoldo Goldbaden in eradicating malaria and Dr. Espiritu Santos Mendoza (no relation) in eliminating polio. He made it possible for more young people to study and advance, for families to live in adequate housing, and for a new spirit of generosity to emerge. But his legacy is not simply the contribution of money or the creation of a wide variety of business and philanthropic institutions. He introduced a new way of thinking about wealth, a new style of doing business, and a new form of philanthropy. Yet to his daughter, Luisa, "He never thought of himself as wealthy." He saw money as "something that can come and go."

Don Eugenio Mendoza is a legend in Venezuela because he made thousands of others the beneficiaries of his success. His activities belied the portrayal by contemporaneous novelists like Graham Greene and V. S. Naipaul of the Latin American businessman who shows no concern for the plight of the poor. In a 1963 interview published in *Reader's Digest*, Mendoza is quoted as saying, "The worker who benefits from capitalism will defend democracy." While directing much of his benevolence to the education of youth, he also argued that, "If you educate a man and he lives in a dump with an empty stomach and no job, he will listen to the first demagogue who offers him a way out." He sought, therefore, to meet a variety of needs at once—education, jobs, proper food, housing. There is a strong message in his conclusion that "nothing less will suffice."

4

Lord Nuffield
England

LORD NUFFIELD WAS A VERY PRIVATE PERSON who put little down on
paper, but his statements, his life-style, and his benevolence tell us much
about the measure of the man. A devout disciple of free enterprise and
private initiative, his motives were less idealistic and his values very different from many of his celebrated colleagues in philanthropy. He had
no children or close relatives to whom he could leave his vast fortune,
and he found the thought of a large windfall for the state at his death an
unpleasant prospect. The fact that he had no heirs was a matter of major
disappointment. He once said, "I have more money than any man can
personally want, and for what it is worth I have a title, but all that I have
been dies when I die. That is my personal tragedy."

Another motive that led to Nuffield's philanthropy was practical
self-interest. According to a letter from one of his lawyers, a primary
purpose in setting up the Nuffield Foundation was to secure "the stability of Morris Motors." Nuffield's aim was to protect in perpetuity the
company he had started as a little bicycle shop and developed into one of
the world's most important business enterprises. Yet it would be a
mistake to draw premature conclusions from the practical, methodical
side of this extraordinary man. Long before he launched his crowning
benefaction, the Nuffield Foundation, he had given away vast sums for
medical, educational, and other purposes. Nuffield once said that giving
away money is pleasant, "but the worry which comes from giving it is

very great . . . the idea that it is easy to give money away is the biggest fallacy in the world." He was generally a systematic, strategic philanthropist, who gave careful thought to his largesse. His many benefactions were not episodic gestures of impulsive generosity, but grew out of his personal experiences and carefully thought-out strategies to achieve specific ends. According to those who knew him, he frequently accompanied his gifts with well-reasoned, eloquently articulated prescriptions as to their use.

It was a long journey from Nuffield's early days as an industrial outsider in the prestigious academic community of Oxford to his becoming a much celebrated "Honorary Alumnus" of the university, and founder of a great postgraduate medical school and a new college bearing his name. The Oxford Dons, who were suspicious, if not opposed, to his early efforts to industrialize their citadel of learning, came to greatly value the Nuffield largesse.

Born William Morris on October 10, 1877, at Worcester, his parents moved to Oxford when he was three. The future Viscount of Nuffield had more than the ordinary youthful interest in bicycles. He was not quite sixteen when he relinquished his formal education and went to work for a local Oxford firm in the bicycle business. At the age of sixteen, he left to set up his own workshop with a working capital of four pounds. By the time he was twenty-three he had begun to construct motorcycles, and by 1912 at the age of thirty-five, he had designed his first car. By 1925 the output of Morris Motors was more than 56,000 cars a year.

It is easy to understand why the announcement of the creation of the Nuffield Foundation in 1943 reported that, "Lord Nuffield desires to make this donation from resources which have been built up through private enterprise, in the essential importance of which he is a key believer."[3] A highly successful entrepreneur who saw himself first as a businessman, he came to regard private enterprise as the best means of promoting national and local well-being. His study and his bedroom, which have been kept intact at Nuffield Place, a few miles west of Oxford, bear witness to his almost total immersion in the principles and practices of private enterprise. Where other men in his time might have surrounded themselves with the works of their favorite philosopher, historian, or novelist, Nuffield's bedroom has a tool cupboard, fully equipped and obviously very well used. A Queen Anne kneehole desk stands in one corner of his study, surrounded by smoking equipment and a wing chair, but his rather spartan bookshelf is filled primarily with mementos and books presented to him by others. The works more obviously of his own choosing relate to business or mechanics. While Morris Motors merged with Austin Motor Company in 1952 to become the third largest in the automobile industry—just below General Motors and Ford—Lord Nuffield, chairman of the board, remained a straightforward, uncomplicated man with simple tastes and a rather ordinary life-style.

The benefactions of this internationally known industrialist were awesome. He gave away much of the money he made—over twenty-eight million pounds before he died. What was the source of his charitable impulse? Who influenced him? Were there other values at work beside the commitment to free enterprise?

Most of Nuffield's charitable donations reflected personal interests.[4] His gifts to hospitals, medical research, and medical schools may have related to his lifelong regret that as a young boy he chose to leave school rather than continue his education and become a surgeon as he had once planned. Some who knew him even suggest that his support for the improvement of the practice of dentistry related directly to bad experiences he had with dentists. His primary passions, however, were those of a patriot. In setting up the Nuffield Trust for the Forces of the Crown, Nuffield wrote a letter to the secretary of state, suggesting that this would "make some personal contribution towards the comfort and well-being of those who are giving up, however temporarily, the ordinary course of their civil occupations and their home surroundings in the service of our country." In 1938 he had played a leading part in an effort to develop an improved aircraft for the British national defense efforts, but had run into difficulties with the Air Ministry. Yet when war came, he was quick to change over some of the key branches of Morris Motors to full-time war work. He was a patriot, strongly supportive of his country and the young men who went off to battle. Through his private resources he sought to help keep alive the values he felt essential to the nation's spiritual health.

If Lord Nuffield had been a political man—running for political office and exercising political power—he undoubtedly would have opposed the development of the welfare state, preferring the pattern developed in the United States in which foundations and private donors share the burden of social service. But for him this was not an ideological abstraction. He put his money where his convictions and his rhetoric led him. Many of his early benefactions went toward the welfare of his employees. During the depression years of the 1930s he set up a trust for the Special Areas of Great Britain. He was deeply concerned about the growing unemployment in some of the depressed regions, so he empowered the trust to make loans to encourage the establishment of new businesses in those areas.

Looking back on Nuffield's philanthropy, his personal values, and his public vision, there are only a few clues to be found about who influenced him and how the charitable impulse evolved. A chief figure in most of Nuffield's charitable projects was William Goodenough, a banker who, at the remarkable age of twenty-four, had become the local manager for Barclay's Bank in the Oxford area.[5] During the inter-war years, when Nuffield began to dispense large sums of money, mainly for the support of local charities, Goodenough was curator of the Oxford University Chest, chairman of the Oxfordshire County Council, and holder of a wide variety of posts that provided a view of where charitable contributions could be most effectively used.

It was not surprising that Nuffield turned to an involved businessman for advice rather than one of the academics at Oxford. He appears to have had little confidence in the advice of most scholars on practical matters.

Goodenough became chairman of the board of the Nuffield Foundation, where he could be relied upon to safeguard Nuffield's interests.[6] In the early years, however, his greatest service to the foundation appears not to have been in persuading trustees to see Lord Nuffield's point of view, but rather in convincing Lord Nuffield, at the request of the trustees, to consider an alternative to what he originally proposed.[7]

Another man who appears to have had close access and considerable influence in the Nuffield charitable network was William Hyde, who for many years wrote for the *Oxfordshire Notebook* and the *Oxford Times*. Using the pen name of Dr. Jekyll, he established himself as a man of considerable influence in Oxford politics. For a time, he had his own office in the Nuffield headquarters and served as a liaison to many groups with which Nuffield was involved. To the duo of Goodenough and Hyde must be added the name of Leslie Farrer-Brown, who had been secretary of the government's interdepartmental committee on medical schools. He became Goodenough's right-hand man, as together they decided how Nuffield's ideas could be best translated into reality. While Nuffield was a rugged individualist in some ways, his views were not dogmatic. The trio of Goodenough, Hyde, and Farrer-Brown provided advice that appears to have been readily received. Moreover, the Nuffield respect for a particular individual was often the source of his philanthropy.

We know very little about Nuffield's religious life. It is not difficult to assume some correlation between his advocacy and commitment to capitalism and the protestant ethic that drove his Calvinist and Quaker contemporaries. But such a moral and value-laden tie does not necessarily lead to the formal practice of religion.

Religious inspiration for Nuffield's philanthropic motivation must therefore remain largely on the level of conjecture. While he had no children, William Morris married Elizabeth Anstey in 1904 and shared his life with her until her death in 1959. She had a life even more private than his own and exercised no discernible influence on either his business or philanthropic activities. Lady Nuffield's separate bedroom and many of her influences have been retained at Nuffield Place, but they tell very little about her taste, concerns, or social proclivities.

There are few clues in the Morris family background to suggest the motivation behind his philanthropy or the source of his fervent faith in free enterprise. His genealogy is a modest one, descending from several generations of small farmers in Oxfordshire. Morris did not particularly enjoy his schooling as a boy, nor is there any record to show that he was a particularly successful student.[8] The only other education he attempted was an evening class in engineering, but records indicate that he only attended twice.[9] Nuffield was completely self-taught and never came to regard formal higher education as being of any great value for his business career or those of his executives.[10] He was quoted in the *Oxford Times* in 1929 as saying, "I've lived long enough to know that it is not always the men who have expensive education who do things."

What appears to have driven Nuffield in business and in philanthropy was not simply a desire to succeed, or to make a difference, but a desire to be seen to be successful. He had a tremendous self-confidence, what some who knew him describe as "an unwavering faith in his abilities and judgment."[11] Nuffield once wrote, "There are very few types of business which I would not be prepared to tackle with some hope of success, relying entirely on my experience in general."

R. J. Overy, who has written one of the most penetrating analyses of the origin and ambitions of Lord Nuffield, argues that although frugality was one of the keys to his success, material reward was important.[12] "Though he had no definite end in view apart from the desire to succeed at something, success and hard work brought its rewards, and the higher the gains the more Morris enjoyed the material confirmation of his success. Whether he sought his millions or his title no record survives the saying. It is clear that he certainly looked for some kind of status, and status was most easily acquired by money."[13] This seems like an unusually harsh indictment of a man who, in addition to being a great philanthropist, was hard-working, honest, fiercely independent, thrifty, and patriotic, but Overy was not the only one who held this view. "He had a single-minded determination to make his mark on the world," wrote Andrews and Brunner.[14] The farmer's son who was originally an outsider at Oxford and its prestigious academic circles not only changed the face of the city of Oxford, but also won his way into the honors—if not the hearts—of the leaders of the great university as well. His many academic honors included an Hon. D.C.L. Oxon. in 1931, Fellowship of the Royal Society in 1939, and five Honorary L.L.D. degrees. He became Honorary Fellow of three Oxford Colleges (Pembroke, Worcester, and Nuffield) and in 1948 was even made an Honorary Fellow of the Royal College of Surgeons. Overy argues that Nuffield's money enabled him to arrive in British circles and ensured that he should stay there.[15]

While Nuffield was not a heavyweight in government social policy, he did exercise considerable influence on economic policy. During the 1920s he assumed the role of chief spokesman for the automobile industry. As Miles Thomas has written in *Out on the Wing*, Nuffield issued regular statements on the need for protection.[16] Yet his political involvement was not simply to make the economic argument in behalf of national self-interest and the business community; he was equally determined to exclude foreign competition at all costs in order to guarantee a rising market for his product.[17] He proudly announced in the 1920s that his cars no longer had any American parts and chose as the firm's slogan "Buy British and be proud of it." Even the highly respected voice of the *Economist* referred to him as reiterating almost weekly "that it is the patriotic and apparently moral duty of every Englishman to refrain from buying foreign cars."[18] A strong protectionist who persuaded a conservative government to intervene strongly on behalf of the automobile industry, Nuffield spent part of his later years trying to persuade a labor government that intervention in the marketplace was bad public policy and bad political philosophy. He called for a hands-off policy which would permit all manufacturers "to work out their own commercial salvation in their own way, unfettered and unhampered by red-tape, restrictions and regulations."[19] Government intervention was bad when it was in behalf of labor but good when it was in behalf of the industry.

While a strong opponent of labor unions, his benevolence actually began in many ways in his own enterprise. He believed in paying good wages and providing a good work environment. "My experience is that if you look after your men, they will look after you," he was fond of pointing out. While paternalistic, he was highly practical in his approach to corporate responsibility. He wanted his employees to regard him not as a taskmaster, but as someone who provided them with whatever he felt they wanted, whether this applied to facilities, wages, hours worked, or even participation in the firm.[20]

Nuffield's charitable impulse appears to have grown out of pragmatism and patriotism, strong convictions about free enterprise, and a strong commitment to his country. The impact of his largesse in his lifetime is not only legend, but the Nuffield Foundation and some of the other institutions he created continue to have a progressive and significant impact on British society.

The *London Times* eulogized Nuffield at his death in 1963 as a philanthropist whose name would be remembered with those of Carnegie and Rockefeller. His commitment to easing suffering and alleviating the human predicament was unquestionably a driving force for his benevolence, but as Ronald Clark pointed out in *A Biography of the Nuffield Foundation*, "It would be both ingenuous and dishonest to claim that this was the only motive that drove him to action."[21] Whether Nuffield used his wealth to buy social status or simply to contribute to the well-being of the nation he loved, his benefactions helped to further the free enterprise system and to demonstrate that it could be humane.

5

Harry Oppenheimer
South Africa

MANY VISITORS TO SOUTH AFRICA return home enchanted by its lavish hospitality, the natural beauty of its wine country and beaches, and its gracious living. The image they form is likely to have been greatly influenced by the South African Foundation, founded by Harry Oppenheimer and several colleagues to present a positive picture of South Africa to the world.

Meanwhile, there is another South Africa. It is well-hidden from the highly visible centers of progress, but populated by 24 million blacks who live on 13.7 percent of the land. The second South Africa exists under the dominance and determination of a small white minority (about 4.8 million) occupying 86.3 percent of the land and buttressed by an economic and political system designed to maintain separate development and to achieve a separate destiny. The Commonwealth Eminent Persons Group on Southern Africa (including the former Prime Minister of Australia and the former head of the Conservative Party in Britain) returned from a fact-finding visit in 1986 to describe what they saw as "awesome in its cruelty." Working with blacks to ameliorate the impact of apartheid is the Urban Foundation, also created by Harry Oppenheimer.

Oppenheimer, former chairman of Anglo American, the largest industrial corporation in South Africa, is identified as much with his philanthropy as with his business dealings. He has spent a lifetime in the eye of the South African hurricane. In his farewell speech to head-office staff upon his retirement from business, he said, "We have to believe, and by our practices demonstrate, that the pursuit of business efficiency and the search for a free and just society are not contradictory objectives, but in fact two aspects of the same thing—two sides of the same coin."

Oppenheimer is himself a contradiction to many, including both sides in South Africa. He was the driving force in getting many of his business colleagues to support the Urban Foundation, which describes its goals as "to improve the quality of life of South African communities, particularly in an urban context ... thereby to contribute to the establishment of a society founded upon justice and the explicit recognition of the dignity and freedom of individuals." The foundation announced in 1980 that its fundamental aim was "real structural change ... a system from which discrimination based on color has been eliminated."

But the Oppenheimer who is the heart and soul of the Urban Foundation is also the major architect of the growth and expansion of the diamond industry that has become an international symbol of the dual realities of South African life. Anglo American employs more than 150,000 workers and virtually controls the world's diamond market. While he has bankrolled a large number of efforts to improve the economic plight of black South Africans, Oppenheimer's philanthropy has been criticized by some as a pacifying cosmetic, seeking greater flexibility in the apartheid system so as to make more effective use of black labor.

A regular critic of apartheid, Oppenheimer has probably done more than anyone else to fuel the economic machine upon which the strength of white supremacy depends.[22] English-speaking, Jewish, and a capitalist, he also arouses many of the deepest resentments in Afrikaners of fundamentalist Christian farming stock.[23] Yet, while his loyalty is occasionally questioned by some Afrikaners, those in political power respect his economic muscle at home and his efforts to promote South Africa abroad.

Harry Oppenheimer was born on October 28, 1908, in the diamond city of Kimberley. His father founded Anglo American, the business organization Harry presided over with such skill that it is now not only the largest combine in South Africa but also a major transnational corporation with business holdings throughout the world, including the United States.

The roots of the Anglo American Corporation date back to 1886 during the diamond rush in Kimberley. Cecil Rhodes was the first to take advantage of the new diamond finds, forming the De Beers Company, which he named after two brothers on whose land one of the local mines was found. By 1890, after a series of owners' struggles and with the help of the Rothschilds, Rhodes found himself sitting atop a mining empire. Cecil Rhodes died in 1902, the year that Harry Oppenheimer's father, Ernest, arrived in Kimberley from London and started a career in mining. He eventually formed the Anglo American Corporation and became director and leading shareholder of De Beers.

In speaking of his father, Harry Oppenheimer describes him as a man who successfully met the problems of his time and left behind him a legacy that is "as great a share of immortality as a modest man should ask for on earth." The young Oppenheimer was educated in England, where he attended the Charterhouse School and Oxford University, earning a degree in politics, philosophy, and economics. He returned home to join his father's firm in 1931 and later served in the military. After returning to Anglo American as managing director, he spent ten years as a member of the South African Parliament.

Oppenheimer became well known as a member of the respected opposition in Parliament, but when his father died in 1957 he resigned his seat to devote full time to his business responsibilities. While he continued to speak out on public issues, he said at one point, "I don't think that one ought in one's capacity as a head of a big public company to plunge into the details of party politics, but I think if you are running a large company in what is, after all, still a comparatively small country, you can't help finding yourself operating in the gray area where politics and business mix." Oppenheimer's attempts to influence public policy have been a natural extension of his efforts to establish a better society in South Africa. He has used both his resources as a wealthy private citizen and his clout as a business executive to improve living conditions for non-whites through housing, education, and social service programs. He also played a leading role in persuading the government to allow blacks to own property in urban areas and to abolish the Pass Laws, which restricted their movement and required them to carry an identity card at all times.

As a corporate executive, Oppenheimer was an early champion of corporate responsibility, calling for "black labor equality with white labor," and often repeating his father's credo that, "The aim of the corporation is to make profits for the shareholders, but to do so in such a way as to make a real and permanent contribution to the welfare of the countries in which it operates." Oppenheimer inherited both his father's business acumen and his commitment to responsible corporate behavior. At both Anglo American and De Beers, he established a Chairman's Fund to finance a broad range of education, research, cultural development, and charitable projects. The annual budget was tied directly to profits, with Anglo American contributing about one percent of its dividends and the mines slightly less. The philosophy that guided his corporate philanthropy was that a project should not rely on permanent subsidization and should have a self-multiplying long-term effect on the development of new thinking— although the project itself could have a limited life. When asked how he justified the fund to corporate shareholders, he answered that shareholders expect company directors to preserve their assets as well as provide a more immediate return on their investments. The Chairman's Fund serves that objective by contributing to the preservation of a stable society.

Under Harry Oppenheimer's direction, Anglo American became a giant conglomerate with holding companies and subsidiaries in every major market in the world. When three prominent Americans were appointed in 1981 to the board of directors of an American subsidiary, the Amcon Group, its chairman announced that this was part of an effort on the part of Anglo American to be seen as a "serious long-term investor" in the United States. The new directors included Cecil Andrus, who had served as Secretary of the Interior in the Carter Administration, Stansfield Turner, the former CIA Director in the Carter Administration, and Irving Shapiro, former chairman of the Du Pont Corporation.

While divestiture in South Africa has been a major objective of anti-apartheid protestors in the United States, the major story may be the expansion of South African capital into the United States. According to the American Committee on Africa, South African firms are into real estate, computers, electrical equipment, Wall Street commodities and investment, and all areas of natural resources. Harry Oppenheimer was an early leader of this advance, with Anglo American using a wide variety of sophisticated organizational techniques to deflect public attention from the South African connection.

But Oppenheimer is now a full-time philanthropist, and most of his beneficiaries are black. Is there a contradiction between his economic position and his philanthropic activities? As one of the richest men in the world, with an empire worth well over $3 billion, some of his critics argue that he should be able to use his power to exert more influence on the ruling Nationalist Party. It should be noted, however, that Oppenheimer is a patriot who is devoted to his country, seeking to occupy the middle ground in a nation that has almost no middle. New moderates like Anglican Bishop Desmond Tutu and his fellow Dutch Reformed clergyman Alan Boesak, for example, have replaced Oppenheimer at the middle. Even the most conservative black leaders, who welcome the Oppenheimer largesse with open arms, are now taking political positions that reflect the frustrations of their community with more than fifty years of largely ineffective nonviolent struggle.

Harry Oppenheimer recognized that South Africa needed more skilled labor in order to maintain its economic growth rate. There was simply not enough white labor to maintain the standard of living that whites had come to expect. The only alternative was to raise the quality of black labor. Yet, while this has been Oppenheimer's constant message, he was not the first, nor the only businessman, to come to that conclusion. As long ago as 1958, a lobby of Afrikaners and English businessman formed the Bantu Wage and Productivity Association (later called the Productivity and Wage Association). The organization's slogan was, "The Bantu should not be looked at as a non-European problem. The Bantu are our national asset."[24] These private sector executives did not pretend to be sentimental or altruistic; they were hard-nosed businessmen who recognized that they could get better work out of their African workers if they were better trained and better paid. It was simply a matter of self-interest.

Needing a more skilled and mobile labor force to service South African industry as the economy has moved from a narrow dependence on mining and agriculture, business has continued to call for increased spending on education, better housing, and the abolition of influx control laws that restricted the ability of Africans to move freely around the country.[25] Through the Urban Foundation, a number of businesses have contributed to black home-ownership schemes and have moved to provide amenities in the black townships that would otherwise be lacking.[26]

There is no doubt that Oppenheimer sees his largesse and the bene-factions of his colleagues in business as enlightened self-interest. The only question is whether his self-interest now demands that he go further than he has thus far been willing to go. He strongly opposes the idea of "one man, one vote" on the grounds that "so-called liberal opinion overlooks the risk, indeed the certainty, that the Afri-cans, who have almost all the same vices as the Europeans, would wish to use political power, if they had it, not primarily to secure good government, but in the interest of black nationalism." He also argues that what the rest of the world must bear in mind is that there are large "white tribes" in Southern Africa and there must be a place in the sun for them as well. At a speech in New York in 1977 to the Foreign Policy Association, Oppenheimer went a little further; he spoke of a need for whites to hold their present "monopoly of power."

This call for the retention of majority power by the minority is in direct contrast to the creed of the South African Freedom Charter adopted at a congress convened by the African National Congress

(ANC) in 1955. The charter states that, "South Africa belongs to all who live in it, black and white, and that no government can justly claim authority unless it is based on the will of all the people."

Oppenheimer opposes apartheid, making frequent calls for its dismantling, but he also opposes revolution, preferring to advocate and actively seek reform. Yet, even black leaders argue that apartheid and reform are basic contradictions. It is, for them, analogous to the slave owner who was willing to reform slavery but not fully abolish it, willing to make it humane but continuing to practice it. Apartheid is a form of social engineering that is achieved and sustained only through force, creating human misery and deprivation. Those who benefit from it may seek to reform it as their self-interest or humaneness dictate, but those who are the victims want the freedom and opportunity to realize their fullest human potential, to live with dignity, and to participate in a government that reflects and represents their will directly.

Thus some of Oppenheimer's colleagues in business have passed him by, taking greater risks than he had been willing to take in order to dismantle the apartheid system. In 1985, for example, a small group of businessmen headed by Oppenheimer's successor at Anglo American went to Zambia to talk to the exiled leaders of the underground ANC about the idea of an all-races convention to work out a new national constitution. There are signs that once-apolitical businessmen who would not dare join Oppenheimer in openly opposing apartheid are now willing to venture into those once-forbidden waters. And once again Anglo American is out in front. Although Oppenheimer once told a gathering of the American Chamber of Commerce in South Africa that no business should offer either moral or material support to the African National Congress, Gavin Reily, the new chairman of Anglo American, has recognized that any solution to the stalemate in South Africa must involve the leadership of the ANC.

Assessing Oppenheimer's motives and his values are difficult. Andrew Young, the Carter Administration's Permanent Representative to the United Nations, described him as a kindred spirit. Introducing him before the Foreign Policy Association in New York in 1977, Ambassador Young said that when he met Harry Oppenheimer, "I felt that I met a man who was dedicated to justice in a land where injustice was perhaps most prevalent, a man who is sensitive and loving despite the requirements of his occupation as a hardheaded, realistic businessman in a very tough economic situation, a man who has proven his sensitivity as well as his economic ability in a climate where it is difficult to do that on a nonracial basis." The staff of the Urban Foundation, both black and white, insist that while they are not the only game in town, they are an important and necessary part of the larger struggle. The same could probably be said of Oppenheimer, who was quoted in the April 1971 *Washington Post* as saying, "If you don't give people a chance to struggle legally for what they want, it creates a climate for illegality. . . . The long term future of South Africa is bleak, but I will do what I can to make black and white equal."

His world has been multiracial even in his social contacts. When his daughter Mary was married in 1965, it was reported that most of the 3,000 guests at the ceremony were black. But they were unable to attend the reception because it was against the law for whites to serve alcohol to blacks on white premises. Oppenheimer's wife Bridget shares his views, as reflected in her multi-racial entertaining at their home in Johannesburg. On the grounds of their estate is the Brenthurst Library, which houses a collection of rare African books and unpublished manuscripts, which they are proud to preserve. They are equally proud of their farm near Kimberley, Harry's birthplace, where they breed some of the finest racehorses in the country. Harry likes to read (in four languages), collect paintings, and ride horseback when he is not preoccupied with preventing his country from stumbling into a bloodbath.

There are many stories about Oppenheimer philanthropy: after local health authorities condemned a school's lavatory facilities, the Dean of Pretoria, the Very Reverend Mark Nye, was reluctant to go again to the community's primary benefactor, but after ten minutes with Harry he emerged with six new lavatories. A group of men approached Harry for support of a worthy project, but he committed only on the understanding that they would raise half of the funds elsewhere. When they returned successful a couple of days later, he asked if they would mind telling him who had agreed to match his gift. One of them answered, "Not at all, we are getting it from your wife."

Harry's father, Ernest, was also known for his largesse, making numerous grants to educational institutions and supporting a number of needy students. Harry has also put considerable money into education, but he has done so because he sees education as a cultural weapon in the war for the South African mind and in the battle for continued economic advancement. He has set up various trust funds for educational purposes, together with the Ernest Oppenheimer Memorial Trust and the Chairman's Fund.

Harry Oppenheimer's mother, who was the daughter of a wealthy member of the London Stock Exchange, also had a history of involvement in humanitarian efforts. With her husband Ernest, she played an active part in organizing soup kitchens for those out of work in Kimberley during a time of high unemployment. Ernest was also elected to the Kimberley Council, where he used the platform to present a list of the many wrongs he thought the council should set right. Harry was thus born into a family that was immersed in public life and whose members were highly respected for their humanitarianism.

Despite Oppenheimer's extensive contributions to public causes to benefit blacks and his willingness to take on the Afrikaner political establishment when others were fearful, he may be remembered as much for the conditions in South African mines as for his private generosity and public dissent. While far ahead of other miners in his approach to corporate responsibility, he is, nevertheless, associated with mine conditions that are sometimes compared to the forced-labor factories next to Nazi concentration camps. Moreover, as more and more blacks become radicalized by the lack of any real progress in dismantling apartheid, his past contributions are being readily forgotten by protest leaders who are younger and more restless than the generation he has known.

What, then, is the Oppenheimer legacy? One may quarrel with his social vision and political positions—as both Africans and Afrikaners have done—but his benefactions speak for themselves. In addition to the large sums he has distributed to benefit blacks in South Africa, he has also been active in other southern African countries, often underwriting the cost of sending doctors to hospitals in Swaziland and elsewhere. His motive for some of his benevolence is clearly enlightened self-interest, but he seems also to have taken a step into disinterested philanthropy, supporting projects and programs, fostering ideas and ideals, that go far beyond the mere maintenance of stability and the enhancement of productivity. Moreover, he has no illusions about the potential and limits of private philanthropy in support of social change. Some of the organizations he supports may be considered less progressive and less credible than others in the South African black community, but even his critics acknowledge that among the myriad strategies and options for South Africa, there is a place for pragmatic, middle-of-the-road approaches that can enlist conservative economic and political leaders who might not otherwise be involved.

Harry Oppenheimer has made a major contribution to the development of a strong voluntary sector that seeks to build a network of well-trained South African leaders in the context of viable indigenous institutions and organizations. This may well be the matrix out of which the ingredients of a new political regime will be formed, along with a transformed social and cultural reality.

PART TWO

The Religious Imperative

INTRODUCTION

The Religious
Imperative

RELIGION SOMETIMES HAS BEEN USED to legitimate personal predilections, to validate the distribution of political and economic power, and to give transcendent meaning to the personal values and styles of the wealthy and influential. This is the religion Karl Marx described as the "opiate of the masses," an instrument of exploitation and injustice. But religion correctly understood and rightly practiced has also been a protest against oppression and a commandment to eliminate suffering. This is the religion that has been a factor in humankind's perception of obligations and duties since the dawn of human history.

Although varied in beliefs and practices, the major common element in many diverse expressions of religion has often been the idea of a moral imperative, a requirement to be or do something that sets adherents apart from all others. While anthropologists claim that many primitive religions were not much more than exercises through which the tribe worshipped its collective being, later religions tended to develop and promote a value system with a very special form of idealism. That is, they sought behavior based on a conception of transcendent purpose. Some religions, and the disparate communities of faith they spawned, defined the religious imperative as maintaining the established social order or recreating a past utopia. Others affirmed a requirement to change the social order to a particular vision of what it should be. The first notion usually emphasized a return to a model of utopia located somewhere in the past. The latter sought to build a utopia in the future. It was the members of the second group who were more likely to identify with the aspirations and needs of an oppressed people or individuals on the margins of society. The imperative to lend aid, solace, and comfort, and even create a new social order, has usually had its source in an "act of revelation" in which the deity or his prophet was believed to have made known his will.

The semitic religions—Islam, Judaism, and Christianity—have more formally emphasized charity as a moral imperative, but echoes of a religious injunction can be found elsewhere. Confucius saw benevolence as worth more than "water or fire." The scriptures of Theravada Buddhism describe charity as a way in which "man and woman alike can store up a well-hidden treasure." It goes on to suggest that "a wise man should do good—that is the treasure that will not leave him." The Koran, the sacred book of Islam, adds a different twist, emphasizing the good that the recipients of charity bestow on the giver. The poor are told to "take alms, so that you may thereby purify and sanctify them." Mohammed even made a distinction between charitable giving in the lifetime of the donor and at death. He suggested that "a man giving in alms one piece of silver in his lifetime is better for him than giving one hundred when about to die." Religious injunctions have also fortified the idea of civic stewardship. Even those philanthropists who acted out of other than religious motives defined civic obligation in a cultural context largely shaped by the moral imperatives of religion. The American model of the Christian gentleman providing charitable relief as part of his moral and civic duty has its counterpart in the Parsi who collected alms for the *punchayet* to distribute to the needy in Parsi communities; the Moslem who believed that *zakat*, contributing to the needs of deserving persons, was one of the five obligatory virtues of Islam; and the Jew whose moral tradition is dominated by the concept of *tsedakah*, the notion that charity is an obligation.

It is not surprising that in both Arabic and Hebrew the word for justice came to be used for alms, for the religious imperative often went beyond sentimental acts of charity, which sought to contain poverty, to include a calculated generosity, which sought to eliminate it.

The three philanthropists in this chapter felt strongly the moral imperative of their religious traditions. One was a Quaker, another a Parsi, and the third a Christian Evangelical, but they shared a common idealism that led them to use their wealth to serve a transcendent purpose. They differed greatly in time and culture, but they all saw themselves as called into a special relationship not only with family and friends, but also with strangers scattered throughout their homelands or across the face of the earth.

6

Angela Burdett-Coutts
England

IT IS SURPRISING that so little is known of Angela Burdett-Coutts. Her benevolence is legend and her life story a drama unto itself. Her career as a philanthropist covered nearly three-quarters of the turbulent Nineteenth Century, touched several continents, and mitigated distress throughout the world. Her span of life and her sphere of influence paralleled that of Queen Victoria. And, not surprisingly, those who benefited from her largesse thought of her in royal terms, dubbing her "the Queen of the Poor."

In the written histories of the Victorian era, Angela Burdett-Coutts is often only a footnote cast in the shadows of Charles Dickens, Henry Irving, William Gladstone, and Benjamin Disraeli, but in her own time she loomed larger than life. Biographers reported that when she attended services at St. Stephen's Church, Westminster, the congregation stood as they would to the queen. A local magazine, in describing her appearance at the Westminster Technical Institute in 1894, wrote that, "When her Ladyship stood up to commence, the ovation was simply tremendous.... No greater respect could have been paid to majesty itself."[1]

The story of Angela Burdett began in 1837, the year King William died and Victoria became Queen of England. It was the year that Angela inherited the vast fortune of her banker grandfather, Thomas Coutts. A young lady of twenty-three, Angela did not have Victoria's pedigree nor any other claim to distinction. Yet, in 1907, the *London Times* suggested that it was "mainly to her example the modern conception of judicious charity is due."

Charitable giving was part of a long aristocratic tradition in England, but Angela set a new standard. While others gave to the poor, she sought to go to the roots of poverty. Not only was her charity without condescension, but she brought a shrewd, businesslike professionalism to her passion. Her father had taught her that great means demanded a great cause, so she made a career of philanthropy. Tutored by Charles Dickens, she discussed theology with William Gladstone and was a close personal friend of the Earl of Shaftesbury and the Duke of Wellington. But while she valued and was inspired by their insights, she was her own person, the key figure in her philanthropic activities. The ideas for the projects she funded often originated with her. Dickens served for several years as the administrator of her charitable giving, but she is reported to have personally read as many as 400 letters a day.

To understand why Angela broke with the "lady bountiful" tradition and embarked on her own brand of "judicious charity," it is necessary to understand the ideas and ideals that shaped her benevolence. She was a solitary child. The youngest of four sisters and a brother, she had an affinity for older people and was especially close to her father, Sir Francis Burdett. His passion for the underdog left a lasting impression on young Angela.

Francis Burdett was born in 1770. While his childhood was undistinguished, his peers regarded him as something of a firebrand. Even as an adult, he made other people uncomfortable, promoting ideas and practicing politics that differed from the Victorian orthodoxy of his era. His wife and in-laws were greatly disturbed by his passion for what they regarded as radical politics. Yet, his father-in-law bought him a seat in Parliament. In his maiden speech he came to the defense of the Irish, attacking the oppression of an "enslaved and impoverished people by a profligate government." His wife was so disturbed by his obsessions that she retreated into imaginary illness and became a chronic invalid. Sir Francis wrote to his father-in-law that "the best part of my character is a strong feeling of indignation at injustice and oppression and a lively sympathy with the suffering of my fellows."

Angela not only inherited her father's zeal, but she lived in the shadows of a family tradition of controversy and scandal. Grandfather Coutts, who was a highly respected banker, had startled Victorian society with not only his financial tenacity but his social audacity. At the age of eighty, only a few days after the death of his first wife, he married Harriet Mellon, a young actress less than half his age. To the surprise of no one, Harriet's stepdaughters received her with hostility and resentment. The press ridiculed her and while she and her husband dined with nobility and other members of the moneyed class, she remained the target of gossip.

When Thomas Coutts died, he left his entire fortune to his new wife, causing family resentment of Harriet to multiply. Now a widowed woman of considerable wealth, she indulged herself in food, drink, and a luxurious life-style. A few years after her husband's death she married the Duke of St. Albans, a man half her age. This presented her with social status to match her wealth. Angela was thirteen at the time, but the ease with which she related to adults caused her to become a favorite of Harriet, who was now the Duchess of St. Albans. Angela was a good listener and Harriet a great talker.

In addition to her enjoyment of a luxurious life-style, Harriet engaged in the charitable activities that had come to be expected of wealthy Victorians. She gave money to the poor, set up soup kitchens, and responded to individual cases of hardship. These activities did not go unnoticed by young Angela, who began at an early age to doubt the efficacy of stop-gap charity. Later she also questioned the publicity that surrounded Harriet's philanthropy, often preferring to be the "lady unknown" on the charity lists.[2]

The bond that developed between Harriet and her granddaughter was curious but not especially threatening to other members of the family. The aging duchess and the gawky teenager seemed to be an incompatible duo, but they took driving trips together and generally ignored the family feud. When Harriet died, however, and left her whole family fortune to Angela, the family was outraged. Even Angela's father, the political radical with the passion for the underdog, responded with such anger that Angela had to take temporary refuge with a former governess.

Angela, at the age of twenty-three, found herself an enormously wealthy public figure. Although forty years later she was to adhere to the idiosyncratic family tradition of marrying someone half her age, she did not encourage the many young Victorians who were eager to gain her affection. Her main concern was spending her income in a socially responsible fashion. She took the surname Coutts—as mandated in Harriet's will—and set out to make a new life for herself. But the heaviest part of her inheritance was the estrangement from her family. She provided a generous allowance for her mother and sisters, but continued to live alone.

The problem of what to do with her wealth preoccupied Angela. A deeply religious person, she believed that her fortune was divinely bestowed and should be administered responsibly. It was her childhood governess, Hannah Meredith, who had taught her about religion and instilled in her an unquestioning childlike faith and devotion to the Church of England. Miss Meredith, who postponed her impending marriage to remain with Angela when she moved out of the family home, remained the most important person in her life.

The religious creed that shaped Angela's view of the moral responsibilities of wealth was that of the Evangelicals, with their piety, earnestness, and commitment to the service of God and man. Evangelicalism's concern with the saving of the individual soul appealed to Angela's private nature, while the emphasis on social responsibility struck a chord with her already developed sense of duty. She had not known John Wesley, the leader of the Evangelical Revival, who died in 1791, but she would have been right at home as a member of the Evangelical group he and his brother formed at Oxford. Like the early Wesley, she was loyal to the Church of England but sought to infuse into it a new spirit of social responsibility. Evangelicalism had now spread to the middle and upper classes. Men like Lord Shaftesbury, who led a movement to improve the treatment of the insane and the working conditions of the poor, sought to give Victorian England a new moral creed. William Gladstone, one of the most famous British political leaders of the 1800s, was an outstanding churchman who wrote several books on theology. His strong moral commitment led him to use his three terms as prime minister as a bully pulpit to preach reform in the political relationship to Ireland. While his attempts to improve the plight of the Irish were largely unsuccessful, his moral fervor touched philanthropists like Angela.

It was not surprising that Angela's earliest forms of benevolence were directed toward the church. In memory of her father, she financed the construction of St. Stephen's Church, Westminster, including the schools and vicarage, which served the constituency her father represented for thirty years. She did so much for the Church of England that it was once observed that, had she been Roman Catholic, she would have been canonized "St. Angela." David Owen, in his monumental work on English philanthropy, wrote that no other woman below the rank of queen had done so much for the church. In addition to her formidable gifts to the various branches of the Church of England, she founded and endowed the colonial bishoprics of Capetown, South Africa and Adelaide, Australia as well as the bishopric of British Columbia. Always remembering those on the margins of Victorian society, she built a church in a poor section of Carlisle completely at her own expense.

The next great influence on Angela, in some ways rivaling the hold of the church, was Charles Dickens. While one of the most popular writers of his time, Dickens busied himself with various charities and used his novels for social criticism—attacking materialism, selfishness, greed, false humanitarianism, the social-climbing rich, and the neglect of the downtrodden. Angela first met Dickens when he was a 23-year-old reporter achieving notoriety for his burning hatred of social injustice.[3] Over the years, their friendship became especially close and his counsel highly regarded. Some observers attributed the broadening of Angela's philanthropic horizon, beyond the church work in which she was first engrossed, to Dickens.[4] He was, according to his biographer, "not only the creative imagination behind many of Miss Coutts' efforts, but their directing force and executive arm."[5]

This is probably an overstatement of Dickens' influence on the proud, headstrong Angela, but her addiction to philanthropy was without doubt enhanced by their relationship. The nature of Dickens' influence can be gleaned from his letters, many of which make as delightful reading as his celebrated novels. In one letter he wrote, "Mr. Tolfrey is not a fit subject for your generous aid, but with a small sum, my dear Miss Coutts, I think I can do on your behalf, an infinitely greater service." He went on to recommend that 30 pounds "would be like help from heaven."[6]

Dickens directed Angela's focus away from the church and toward the poorest members of society. Poverty in England had always existed. Many believed with Wilberforce that the "lowly paths of the poor had been allocated to them by the hand of God," but charitable work came to be regarded as a duty. While debates raged about the deserving and undeserving poor, Dickens and Angela made no such distinction. They were more interested in identifying the causes of poverty and contributing to long-term solutions. At the age of twelve, Dickens had worked in a London factory pasting labels on bottles of shoe polish. He held the job for only a short time, but the misery of that experience left a lasting impression. He used his skills as a keen observer of the human condition to denounce urban slums, poor sanitation, and the Crimean War. But many of his contemporaries saw the real evil to be not poverty, but pauperism. In 1834, three years before Angela's inheritance launched her career in philanthropy, Parliament had passed the Poor Law, which abolished the system of paying allowances out of parish funds to paupers and set up in its place the hated union workhouses. Angela strongly disapproved of this new law, which was so inhumane in its application, and so chose to work closely with Dickens toward social reform. The cause of poverty concerned her as much as the cause of evil concerned philosophers and theologians.

The times called for a new approach to the problems of the poor, a new philanthropy that understood the changing currents of social reform, rather than public benevolence or private charity, which primarily supported social service. The forces creating a new industrial society and greatly influencing social values also affected the motives and methods of Angela's philanthropy. She saw, better than most, the difficulty of transferring to the new, growing urban population the approaches, institutions, and network of relationships that made rural England a society largely accommodating to the charitable activities of benevolent wealth. Moreover, social problems that had not disturbed the rural philanthropist living in isolated elegance now thrust themselves on the doorsteps of the urban elite. Education and training that had served well enough in a rural peasant milieu were clearly inadequate for the emerging industrial order. Health and housing also took on a new significance.

Among the projects to which Angela devoted herself was her work with "women of the streets." Disturbed by the nightly parade beneath her window, she proposed to set up a home that would restore wayward girls to health and respectability. Her good friend the Duke of Wellington was less than enthusiastic, writing to her that "experience, as well as the information to be derived from statistical works, have taught us that there is but little if any hope of saving in this world that particular class of unfortunates to whom you have referred.... I am afraid that it has been found that there are irreclaimables of that particular class who earn their bread by the commission of the offence."[7]

Encouraged by Charles Dickens, Angela went on with her plans to restore women of the streets to respectable and productive lives. As a champion for "fallen women" and in many of her other projects, Angela was ahead of her time. With regard to the rights of women in general, however, she was very much a product of her time. She personally enjoyed a degree of independence not normally available to Victorian women, but her views on the role and rights of women were rather conventional. On this issue she believed in "the immutability of the existing social order."

Angela Coutts' benevolence covered myriad causes, but she seems to have had a special commitment to child welfare and education. Childless herself, and with limited education, she came to regard untutored and neglected children as a wasted national resource. Her concerns were well suited to Dickens' investigation of the Ragged School. According to David Owen, once she became a patron of the Ragged School union, she entered naturally into other stages of work to promote the welfare of children. She helped to form shoe brigades for boys salvaged by the Ragged Schools and supported the development of the Destitute Children's Dinner Society, which she served for many years as president. This latter group was a novel auxiliary of the Westminster Ragged School, in which penny dinners were served in fifty centers. Angela believed deeply that the dignity of the poor was maintained when they were able to contribute to their own support rather than relying completely on charity. Yet, when the neglected children in the dinner society could not come up with their penny or the centers could not become self-supporting, she picked up the cost.

Like Dickens, the Duke of Wellington was also a close confidant of Miss Coutts. When she wasn't visiting him at Apsley House, they were exchanging warm and admiring letters. He had at first watched the career of his neighbor, the Duchess of St. Albans, with amused tolerance, but he and Angela soon became deeply attached to each other. The Duke was aging and his influence had waned, but he was still a popular and dashing figure on the social circuit. Dickens was often traveling or engaged in other pursuits, and Hannah Meredith, the former governess who became Angela's constant companion, had finally married her beloved Dr. Brown. Thus it was the Duke who gained more and more of Angela's attention and esteem. She consulted him on many of her charitable activities—and even supported some of his pet projects—but she rarely took his advice. He was not only dubious about her fallen women project, he was also more interested in the traditional charities of the Victorian elite. Yet, while Angela's head was with Dickens, her heart was with the Duke. To his surprise, she proposed marriage. She was thirty-three at the time and he was seventy-seven. His rejection strengthened, rather than weakened, their friendship.[8] Even Queen Victoria was relieved.

In his novel *Bleak House,* Dickens contrasted Mrs. Jellyby's "telescopic philanthropy" that could take an interest in nothing nearer than Africa with Mrs. Pardiggle, the "moral policeman" who concentrated her energies at home. Angela brought Mrs. Jellyby and

Mrs. Pardiggle together. Her concern for the downtrodden was international. She inherited her father's concern for the Irish, and set up relief centers during the great famine where goods could be purchased cheaply. She supported emigration to Canada and offered financial backing for Livingstone's expedition. She supplied funds for churches in South Africa, cotton gins in Southern Nigeria, and even provided hospital equipment and nurses during the 1879 war with the Zulus.

The range of the charitable activities of this woman who rivaled Queen Victoria, Charles Dickens, and William Gladstone as the dominant figure of the Victorian era can be seen in the support of her friend Rajah Brooke of Sarawak. Among other things, she funded the purchase of military supplies for him to defend his rule of this kingdom in the jungles of Malaysia and tried to persuade the British government to keep Sarawak in English hands. The Rajah responded to her generosity by leaving Sarawak in trust to her. The kingdom became independent in 1964.

It is easy to over-romanticize the contributions of this remarkable woman, if only because she has been so neglected by historians and social biographers. But as with most legends, there are the deeply human longings and failures that remind us of the humanity of those whom we are tempted to idolize. There was clearly a touch of the eccentric in Angela, as typified by her singular marriage at the age of sixty-seven to her American secretary forty years younger. The ceremony was complete with little bridesmaids, bridal dress, and veil, causing Queen Victoria to write in her journal of that "poor foolish old woman Burdett-Coutts [who] looked like his grandmother."

There was also an element of pathos in Angela's life. Despite what appeared to be a happy, varied, and fulfilled life, she was essentially an isolated person, isolated by her estrangement from her family, naturally insulated by her wealth and position, and set apart by what appeared to be a wariness of close contacts. Her unconventional pursuit of the Duke and her marriage to the youngster, Ashmead Bartlett, surely point to something lacking in her private life. The relationship with Hannah Meredith remains something of a mystery. Whether it was conventional or sexual is not the point; what matters is that it was one of emotional dependence and devotion.

Did all this affect Angela's philanthropy? It almost certainly did, but there is no denying that she was unique among Victorian philanthropists, tackling her charitable activities with method and imagination. She gave to emergency relief when she felt it necessary, but she made her mark in searching for long-term remedies. When she sought to help the unemployed, she assumed that they wanted to work and supported job creation. Her most significant contribution, however, may have been an act of moral rebellion, her rejection of the prevailing view that those who were poor, downtrodden, or without work were lazy, lacking in moral fiber, or incompetent. The *London Times* called it judicious charity. Another equally appropriate description would be practical philanthropy. It may be that charity is the marriage of poverty with abundance, but for Angela Burdett-Coutts philanthropy was the will—the daring—to go beyond charity.

7

Jamsetji Nusserwanji Tata
India

IN 1904, THE YEAR that Mohandas K. Gandhi came to public attention on the Phoenix Farm in South Africa, Jamsetji Tata was on
his deathbed in Germany. The Indian artist and poet Tagore was
contributing to a new spirit of renaissance, and the Indian National
Congress was already active. But while many of India's intellectuals
and political activists were still dazzled by the administrative, tech-
nological, and cultural achievements of foreign rulers, Jamsetji Tata
was to be remembered as the man who first began to chip away
at local apathy and acceptance of the second-class status imposed
by British colonial rule. His initial struggle was economic, but his
subsequent contributions came to embrace all of Indian life.

Jamsetji's cousin, J. R. D. Tata, remembered him as a man who
was restless in his search for new ideas. "When others thought first
in terms of political action on behalf of India, Jamsetji understood
the full potential for his country of the industrial revolution in the
West. He wanted India to be independent but also to grow strong
industrially—then an uncommon idea."[9]

Writing about his travels through India, John E. Frazer put Jamsetji's
wealth and influence in perspective: "In Bombay, I stayed at one
of India's finest hotels, the Taj Mahal. It was opened by Jamsetji
in 1903. I flicked on the light switch—and power furnished by a
Tata hydroelectric company lighted the room. The room was air-

conditioned by Volta's Ltd.—a Tata-associated company. I bathed with a fragrant dark-green soap from Tata Oil Mills, donned a white bush shirt of cotton woven by a Tata textile mill."[10] Frazer continued: "When I travelled on the Indian Railways, my train was hauled by a 99-ton steam locomotive built by the Tata Engineering and Locomotive Company Ltd. I flew to England from Bombay aboard a jet of Air India International, now government-owned but established by Tata."

The Tata industrial combine also produced paints, perfumes, pesticides, fertilizer, automobiles, trucks, cement, and salt from seawater. From his mines came coal, chromite, iron, and manganese. Yet, Jamsetji is best remembered not so much for his business success or his affluence; his stature in Indian society, then and now, came from his belief that wealth was merely a means toward an end. The end was the good of the nation, its economic advancement, its prosperity. His countrymen remember him as a man who "left a legacy not merely of opportunity but also of duty."[11] It was the use of his profits for the public good that caught their imagination and later earned for him and his family the title "the Rockefellers of Asia." The late Jawaharlal Nehru, who served as the first Prime Minister of India from 1947 to 1964, described him as "far-sighted, a man respected throughout India as a great Indian."

It is somewhat ironic that a descendant of a long line of Parsi priests came to play such a significant role in the economic and social policy of the nation rather than its religious life. After all, Navsari, where Jamsetji was born in humble circumstances in 1822, had been the center of Zoroastrian culture for 800 years. The colonies of refugees who settled there after their flight from persecution in Persia had worked hard to maintain the area as a citadel of orthodoxy. But they lived in constant fear of defilement from contact with Hinduism, and engaged in endless theological controversies about the purity of their creed. It is quite likely, however, that Jamsetji was exposed very early in life to the practice of almsgiving, one of the Parsi traditions that remained untainted.

As early as 1669 the Parsi faithful in India had created an institution for its members' benefit. In accordance with the duality of good and evil inherent in Zoroastrianism, this organization, known as the *punchayet,* initially meted out justice to social and religious wrongdoers in the community. It later evolved into a strictly charitable entity, receiving donations from and dispensing relief to Parsi communities.[12]

Jamsetji thus grew up in an atmosphere of traditional piety; its charitable ethic and moral theology left a lasting impression on his character. He had not only been exposed regularly to Parsi charity, but he himself had been the beneficiary of the Tata Trusts established by his father Nusserwanji. While these early experiences of communal concern were limited to the immediate family or the religious community, later the young Tata was to develop a much broader vision. Meanwhile, he learned to work hard and developed at an early age an interest in commodities, markets, and exchange as well.[13]

His early life was lived in accordance with the religious rites of the Parsi. He was ordained a priest, but a fortune-teller singled him out as a boy who would travel, become rich, and live in a big house in Bombay. He received no formal schooling until he was thirteen. Yet he developed a passion for reading that was both wide-ranging and encyclopedic. Strongly opposed to narrow specialization, he was convinced that, since knowledge did not stand still, the educated person needed to remain open to new ideas and adaptable to shifting circumstances. He graduated from Elphinstone College in 1858, the year the British assumed sovereignty over India. In many ways he remained a student for the rest of his life. When there was a currency crisis, he studied economics; when the bubonic plague was taking its toll in Bombay, he read every available book and pamphlet relating to the various plagues and to the background of the disease.[14]

Described by those who knew him as a man of general culture, the young Tata was known as a lover of fine and beautiful things. Like Winston Churchill, he believed that man shapes his buildings and is, in turn, shaped by them. It was no surprise, therefore, that he developed a keen interest in architecture and city planning.

Jamsetji's first job was in a solicitor's office, but when his first son was born in 1859, increased financial responsibilities led him to join his father's business. He was only twenty years old at the time, but rose quickly in the firm and assumed major responsibilities. His first significant assignment was in Hong Kong, where he established a branch office. After tenure in Shanghai, he returned home at the age of twenty-six an established success in business.

A pioneer in industrial relations, he believed that the keys to efficiency were decent wages, a healthy and supportive work environment, and education. As he accumulated personal wealth and presided over the development of a far-reaching business empire, he gave heavily of his time and fortune toward the building of a new India. He contributed to the construction of schools, hospitals, factories, roads, dams, and railways. But while he was a sympathetic and generous man in every way, he came to believe that, "What advances a nation or a community is not so much to prop up its weakest and most helpless members, as to lift up the best and most gifted so as to make them of the greatest service to the country."[15] His social philosophy was in many ways similar to what W. E. B. Du Bois, the American civil rights leader, called the development of "the talented tenth."

The earliest of Jamsetji's benefactions was the incorporation of an endowment fund for the purpose of lending money to graduates who had passed their examinations with distinction in one of the Indian universities but were interested in continuing their studies in Europe.[16] At first it was intended for the benefit of "young men of his own community but in 1894, its scope was enlarged and made quite catholic by allowing its benefit to all graduates of the requisite attainments of any Indian University."[17]

Tata's earliest form of philanthropy emanated, therefore, from his desire to see the intellect of India developed along new lines of self-help and self-reliance. From the beginning, he believed that philanthropy should be practical and constructive. In a series of tributes to his legacy shortly after his death, Sir Lawrence Jenkins eulogized him as a man whose mind was capable of the largest projects, yet nothing was "too small to interest him. He was at all times ready to assist merit and honest effort. He believed in the capabilities of his countrymen and was ever ready to help in developing their talents."

While Jamsetji Tata was a businessman who used free enterprise to develop and modernize India, he was also a patriot who took interest in the political life of the nation. He was one of the founding members of the leading political association of his time—the Bombay Presidency Association. It was reported that not only was he a founding member but he also induced his aging father to join. It was also well known that he was "a generous contributor to the funds of the British Committee of the Indian National Congress."[18]

Jamsetji made a special effort to avoid the limelight of professional politics, but he did not hesitate to throw himself into a political fight when economic issues affecting the country were involved. Once, when the government introduced stringent financial legislation following a decline in the exchange value of the rupee, he publicly attacked the proposal as "giving with an open hand to those who already had plenty, while taking away from those who scarcely had anything." He went on to caution that, "Whereas the endeavor of the statesmen ought to be to redress the balance of making the poor somewhat less poor, the recent action of the government of India palpably favors the creditor class at the expense of the debtor class."[19]

Though a wealthy man himself, he expressed his solidarity with the chronically poor, arguing that through the new legislation "the government's measures have really imposed an additional tax on the poor whom everybody admitted to be over-taxed already." He continued: "It is the wealthy Indian who has derived advantage from the artificial cheapening of all articles imported from Europe and all gold-using countries."[20]

Thus Jamsetji, an intensely private man with a strong sense of social justice, took on not only the British rulers but members of his own class who stood to benefit from the legislation. It was not surprising, therefore, that he was attacked by an editorial in *The Times of India* as yielding to "the temptation of addressing the native gallery." It was expected that a man of wealth would defend the privileges of wealth. He might even be compassionate enough to provide support for the poor, but certainly not to the disadvantage of his economic class or his personal benefit.

———————

What are we to make of this strong identification with the poor? Was he concerned primarily with the poor in his religious community, or did he include in his embrace all those on the margins of the Indian economy? To understand Jamsetji Tata, we must also understand the tension that was developing in the Parsi community between its unique religious identity and the dawning of a new nationalism. The Parsi priests and their most orthodox followers sought to maintain the distinct religious and cultural identity of Zoroastrianism. In this effort, they had a wide variety of factors in their favor. Their keen features and pale complexion tended to distinguish them from all other Indians as clearly as their religious rites and prayers. Yet, like the Muslims, Christians, and Sikhs, they were caught up in the growing sense of nationalism forced upon the Indian people in part by a common objection to British rule and in part by the emerging sense of peoplehood celebrated by Indian poets and affirmed by Indian politicians.

At the same time that some members of the religious community were merging into a new national mosaic, the Parsis stood out in at least two other important ways: 1) their cultivation and appreciation of education and 2) their tendency, to the lament of the traditionalists, to be more Western in their ways and habits than other indigenous groups.

It was against this background that Jamsetji wrote in *The Times of India* that the Parsi community was "peculiarly suited as interpreters and intermediaries between the rulers and the ruled." Prompted by the earlier editorial attack, he was seeking to clarify his own attitude regarding the special role of the small Parsi community. He went on to acknowledge that "through their peculiar position they have benefitted more than any other class by English rule," but "at the same time it must not be forgotten that much is due from them to the people of this country which gave them shelter for centuries before the commencement of the British rule." As Aryans (non-Semitic Middle-Easterners) who emigrated to India from Persia to escape Moslem persecutions early in the Sixth Century A.D., the Parsis remained grateful for having been provided a new homeland. Predictably, Jamsetji Tata was asserting both his dual identity and his dual loyalty: he was a Parsi, but he was an Indian first. His presence at the birth of the Indian National Congress and his continuing financial support left no doubt about his role in the development and support of the dawning nationalism.

As could be expected, however, Jamsetji in his early years had gravitated toward his family and the Parsi community in the sharing of both the burdens and the benefits of his success. When he returned to Bombay in 1868 after a stint in England, he resumed his acquaintance with many of the young Parsis he had met while abroad. They would regularly meet either at their homes or at a hotel for dinner, or at the local bandstand for informal conversation. As more young Parsis sought to join this respected social circle, Jamsetji, remembering the role of social clubs in England, introduced the notion of a more formal gathering with more permanent quarters. The Elphinstone Club was thus born. At first the elder generation looked aghast at what they thought was merely an imitation of Western practice alien to Indian society, but they soon came to recognize the club's importance in transmittting values and promoting mutual understanding. Elphinstone became an intergenerational gathering place and played a key role in the life and subsequent development of Bombay. But Jamsetji's notion of community soon came to include not simply his living family, his club, and the Parsis, but the workers with whom he saw himself as engaged in a joint enterprise for the national good. The labor situation in India at that time was not good. Absenteeism was unusually high, productivity was low, and workers rarely identified with their employers, mostly companies owned and run by British colonials. But the young Tata, full of determination and eager to modify the prevailing psychology of labor, set out to change all that.

He did three things. First, he tried to improve the factory environment, making his mills safer and more comfortable. Then he introduced incentives to encourage good attendance, good conduct, and good work. In what was undoubtedly regarded as genuine heresy, he began to break down the rigid barriers between workers and managers, providing opportunity for employees of different ranks to meet in nonthreatening situations. The third aspect of his three-pronged approach followed closely on the heels of the second. His new system of bonuses and other gratuity schemes applied to rank-and-file workers as well as to officers. His deep understanding of human nature and his strong social conscience led him to pioneer in many other areas of worker welfare and employee amenities.

As Jamsetji Tata's wealth and influence grew, there seemed to develop a growth in sensitivity to human suffering and a commitment toward improving the lot of the less fortunate. Soon after Jamsetji Tata's death, his friend Sir Lawrence Jenkins, Chief Justice of Bombay, referred to his sympathy as being no "empty phrase," but "a living force," adding, "I myself have seen his eyes fill with tears when speaking of the poor and the hardships of their lives."[21] Sympathy was not his only response, however. Even where his own business interests were involved, Tata refused to take a commercial action that threatened the dignity or endangered the well-being of the poor. Once, when he had an opportunity to buy up the supply of cotton seed and convert it to oil for a large profit, his first concern was with how the poor would feed their cattle if he bought the seed.

A man of deep social conscience, Jamsetji Tata was also a man of extraordinary taste. He delighted in his estates and the quality of their design, upkeep, and libraries, but he took no particular delight in ostentation. While he enjoyed and rewarded quality in others, he never forgot his humble roots in Navsari. That sleepy little town was the seat of an annual Tata family reunion, a week of festivities in which school children were presented prizes and young and old engaged in sports. He also endowed a school and donated a public park there. He knew the value of athletics and social life, but except for sailing, he was not much of a sportsman himself. Jamsetji was a frequent visitor to the Elphinstone Club, but as much to keep it going for the enjoyment of others as for his own pleasure.

His values were undoubtedly influenced by his upbringing as a Parsi, but he was far from orthodox in his religious attitudes. His

travels and his reading clearly enlarged his world view, but his pride
in his heritage and strong sense of nationalism led him to borrow
from the best in the West and to adapt both new ideas and new
technology to the development of modern India. He was a businessman
with a strong social conscience who believed in constructive philanthropy, using private resources to prepare others for self-reliance.

His sense of public responsibility started with his family and embraced the Parsi community, to which he felt a special affinity. It
came to include the workers in the Tata enterprises, the communities
in which he operated facilities, the poor and suffering, and ultimately,
the national community. The House of Tata, which he constructed
out of a strong devotion to enterprise and education, an abundance
of compassion, and a strong national commitment, was one of the
pillars on which modern India was built.

Paramount among Jamsetji Tata's legacy was his establishment
of institutions for organized philanthropy, whereby he sought to go
beyond traditional almsgiving or the strictly communal concern of
the Parsis. The charity-minded Parsis provided relief for the poor
in their religious communities, but neither the wealthy donors who
gave to the *punchayet* nor the trustees who administered it felt the
need for an inquiry into the deeper causes of poverty and destitution.
Moreover, because of their commitment to taking care of their own,
they saw no need to coordinate their charitable efforts with either
nonprofit bodies or government agencies working in the same field.

Jamsetji's larger vision of philanthropy as an instrument of national
development was not a part of the misssion of the *punchayet,* nor
was it part of the theology of the Zoroastrian trustees who sought
and distributed communal largesse. The nonsectarian fund that he
set up in 1892 grew to become the Tata Endowment for the Higher
Education of Indians. Almost every important leader in the post-
colonial civil service, the arts, science, medicine, engineering, and for-
estry benefited from the Tata benefaction. In addition, the funds
he set aside in 1898 for the establishment of the Indian Institute
of Science, later added to by his two sons, now support India's most
important institutions of higher learning and research. Tata Trusts
own more than 80 percent of the stock in the parent firm of Tata

8

Joseph Rowntree
England

A QUIET MAN BY DISPOSITION, Joseph Rowntree rarely made headlines. Yet as an English philanthropist during a period of extraordinary social transformation, he stood against the tide, suspicious of what he described as "the charity of endowment and the charity of emotion." He would have differed strongly with a British Charity Commissioner who observed more than fifty years after Rowntree's death that, "The role of philanthropy is to bind up the wounds of society...to build a new society is for someone else." Joseph Rowntree helped to bind up the wounds of the late Nineteenth and early Twentieth Centuries, but his real interest and his most significant contribution was in building a new society. His principles, his public philosophy, and his philanthropy were all disposed toward that end.

Much of philanthropy is directed toward "remedying the more superficial manifestation of weaknesses or evil," he once wrote, "while little thought or effort is directed toward searching out their underlying causes. It is much easier to obtain funds for the famine-stricken people in India than to originate a searching inquiry into the causes of these recurrent famines. The soup kitchen in York never has difficulty in obtaining adequate financial aid, but an inquiry into the extent and causes of poverty would enlist little support." Rowntree believed that benevolence was likely to be more effective if it was the product of rational analysis as well as emotional feeling.

Born into a Quaker family whose values and life-style were colored by the teachings and beliefs of the Society of Friends, Rowntree was greatly concerned about the uses of wealth. Personally, he had little desire for material possessions. By taste and conviction, he preferred a simple life, once writing a private memorandum to his sons and daughters on the dangers of wealth. He was concerned about what he considered to be the barriers between those on the margins of the economy and those in the mainstream. He feared that if not appropriately used, wealth would "lessen that realizing sense of human brotherhood, which is of such paramount moment to maintain." He cautioned his children and grandchildren not to lose "the sense of the need of cultivating habits of thought for others."

Warning against the potentially negative consequences of wealth, he wrote, "Perhaps the first and most obvious danger is self-indulgence. We know the typical wealthy young fellow, full of himself, thinking a great deal about his convenience and comfort, able to get what he wants without self-denial or strenuous effort, to whom the notion of self-sacrifice is strange, and who has no high ideals of life. These self-concentrated and self-indulgent creatures are neither happy themselves nor do they add to the happiness of others."

A biographer described Rowntree as shrewd, intelligent, and unassuming, a man who "went his own way without heat or haste. He was not a rebel, but he had some of the qualities of a revolutionary. He did not easily accept the status quo in his business or anywhere else."[23]

Oliver Wendell Holmes once said that we are all vehicles in which our ancestors ride. To understand Joseph Rowntree, how his values were developed, and what led him to use his private wealth for public purposes, we need to go back to his formative years in York, the county seat of Yorkshire in northeastern England. He was born on May 24, 1836, above the family shop in the central city. It was a time in which urban areas were largely outside the orbit of the old ruling class, neglected by their natural leaders—developing as best they might, unpoliced, ungoverned, and unschooled.[24] Rowntree's father (whose name was also Joseph) was a product of the Quaker experience of the time in which formal education stopped at the age of fourteen or fifteen. But unlike some of the other self-made businessmen who were on the vanguard of the industrial revolution, many of the Quaker entrepreneurs used their leisure for reading on a scale that would have amazed most scholars. Because of their religious beliefs, however, the Rowntrees and other Quakers could not aspire to matriculation at Oxford or Cambridge. These institutions were closed to religious nonconformists.

The elder Rowntree kept many books in his house above the store, surrounding his children with the key literary works of the time. Parliamentary reports were frequently read aloud at the dinner table. Bible reading after breakfast was a common practice: the Rowntree children were expected to learn a new verse each day. Joseph, Sr. also served on the education committee that governed Quaker schools. He appears to have been a more familiar and approachable parent than many fathers of his time, most of whom tended to follow a rather rigid pattern. He did not subscribe to the theory that children should be seen and not heard.

Joseph's mother, too, was a devout Quaker, but she was also part of a tradition of independent women who enjoyed a high degree of freedom to pursue their own fulfillment. Sarah Rowntree was accustomed to public speaking at a time when most women would not dare address their thoughts even to their own family. If she had to address a meeting of any kind, she always prayed that her words might not be found dull or uninteresting.[25] The Rowntrees entertained on a large scale, but primarily members of the Society of Friends, exposing Joseph to many of the Quaker leaders of his day. When Quarterly Meetings were held in York, men like John Bright, who was an influential member of Parliament, came into the Rowntree orbit. He and the elder Rowntree were allies in several efforts to reform and update Quaker practices. An active Quaker who led the opposition in Parliament to the Crimean War, he was also very concerned with the State of Ireland. He was one of young Joseph's first and earliest heroes.

Another strong influence on the development of Joseph Rowntree's values and his sense of social responsibility was his experience at the Bootham School in York. Like Quaker young men of his time, his formal schooling stopped early, but the five years at the Bootham School were the most important. It was a traditional Quaker institution, but because of its headmaster, John Ford, it was far more progressive than its practice of denying students access to newspapers would imply. This was in keeping with the Quaker practice of isolation, but it was more symbolic than real. The headmaster and his staff encouraged intellectual curiosity and were not afraid to explore student questions in great depth. Ford's belief that Latin and Greek were essential subjects was not revolutionary, but his introduction of science into the curriculum was somewhat radical for his time.

The forty-five students at Bootham were like a family. John Ford believed that a large part of every boy's education took place outside of school, and he expected his staff to be familiar companions of their pupils. Joseph had the kind of inquiring mind that flourished in a school like Bootham. Little is known about his scholastic achievements, but school records indicate that he won a prize for an essay on natural history. He also appears to have been an athlete of sorts, having once won a hotly contested 100-yard race. He was clearly not a long jumper, however, for legend has it that he missed his last summer's cricket match because of a broken leg suffered when he tried to jump a wide ditch.

A prolific reader, Rowntree continued to enjoy and encourage reading for the rest of his life, even establishing a library and a newspaper for his employees. As a boy, he is reported to have read in the quiet of his father's library such works as the novels of Jane Austen and the two books that were the subject of considerable public debate in the English world of his time: Darwin's *Origin of Species* and *Liberty* by John Stuart Mill. He continued to read widely in history and philosophy, but he is remembered for having taught for forty years in the Adult School run by the Quakers in York. The school started out as a regular Sunday morning Bible class, but while retaining the centrality of the scripture lesson, Rowntree taught men much his elder how to read and write.

Joseph Rowntree also enjoyed public debate. As a young man in London, he went off to the gallery of the House of Commons with a sense of excitement and anticipation most young people today reserve for television, movies, or rock concerts. One of his letters to his mother revealed his lifelong fascination with carefully stated and clearly arranged facts as he referred to "the unanswerable arguments and earnest appeals of Mr. Cobden." Additional insight into his personality and his principles can be gleaned from his further statement that "his (Mr. Cobden) case was so strong that ministers knew not how to answer it and had to resort to those appeals which always win approvals, about the 'honor of the British flag', etc." His ancestors for 300 years had been suspicious of high-sounding phrases that sought to appeal exclusively to patriotism. He was not only in that tradition, but according to his biographer, "His conception of honor was far removed from any easy patriotic formula."[26]

In York there was a soup kitchen that Joseph's father had helped to start, but when Joseph in later years talked about dealing with causes rather than with consequences, he could very well have been reflecting his perception in Ireland that soup was not really the answer to poverty.

There was one other experience with poverty that remained imprinted on Rowntree's mind. While many of his Victorian colleagues were engaged in the public debate that sought to make a distinction between the "deserving" and "undeserving" poor, he turned to his belief in the power of clearly articulated and well-arranged facts. Others were interested in determining how to ameliorate the pervasive misery; Joseph was looking for the root causes, how to eliminate them. It was against this backdrop that he began his massive project to gather statistics on poverty and to relate what he found to causes. He attributed the large number of "paupers" to such factors as education and illiteracy. He wrote several essays and delivered key speeches on the subject, arguing that too much of the country's wealth was being spent on armaments and not enough on education. Some of his friends were concerned about how strongly he emphasized his conclusions but few could take issue with his figures on demographics, his analysis of the economy, the national expenditures, and even the export and import figures.

Joseph was thirty now, and his concerns were not the passionate indignation of a young man, but the measured authority of one who had been assembling his facts for half his life.[27] He wrote that it was "a monstrous thing that in this land, rich beyond all precedent, millions of its inhabitants, made in the image of their creator, should spend their days in the struggle for existence so severe as to blight (where it does not destroy) the higher parts of their nature."[28]

Although his was a calm, assured, and well-reasoned voice, even some of his associates in the Society of Friends became concerned when he charged that the social ideals of both the state and the church were out of tune with the realities of the time. Here again one finds the seeds of his philosophy of philanthropy, for it was in his essay on "Pauperism" that he attacked "charity as ordinarily practiced, the charity of endowment, the charity of emotion, the charity which takes the place of justice."

This was not the voice of an idle activist or a naive social reformer. The great fortunes Rowntree later earned were those of a man who knew what it meant to meet a payroll, to worry over a profit-and-loss statement, and to face the competitive challenge of the marketplace. Starting with a little factory staffed by twelve men, Rowntree's business expanded to include over 7,000 employees.

Social beneficence may have been in his blood, but economic struggle was in his bones. He took some very large risks in the cocoa business and eventually reaped some very large rewards, but there were many lean years in between. Through it all he regarded those who worked for him as individual persons first and employees afterwards.

It would serve little purpose here to provide details about the cocoa business, but it is helpful to look at the Rowntree business philosophy. The ideals we find active in his philanthropy were also active in his business practices. He had learned his skills under the benevolent autocracy of his father in the family's small grocery shop. Traces of his approach to owner-management can be found in the early Joseph. Yet he not only changed as circumstances changed, but long before the modern concept of corporate responsibility entered our vocabulary, he was practicing what men like the Olivettis in Italy and later Irwin Miller in the United States came to regard as "enlightened" business management.

In 1885, when the Rowntree business was still marginal and survival was a daily concern, Joseph used his own money to start a library for his employees. His concern for their intellectual and social development led him later to establish a debating society and to arrange and sponsor concerts and other festivities. It is reported that these gatherings were very popular, for there were few entertainments of any sort which working people could afford.[29] He later received considerable attention for the establishment of a company retirement pension and for his concern and contribution to improved housing for his employees. Yet he remained committed to a quality product, recognizing that his first responsibility was to run a successful business.

In 1891, Joseph Rowntree appointed a woman to a management position. He was concerned about the man-made world young women found as they came to his factory at a very early age. He was clearly a pioneer in corporate responsibility, but he saw this as simply an extension of good business practices. The ideals that led him to philanthropy were no different from the ideals that influenced the way he managed his company.

Another influence that made an impression on Joseph Rowntree was the antislavery movement among Quakers and its emphasis on the concept of the freedom and dignity of man. "Moreover, the emergence of that movement occasioned the introduction of two new methods of social agitation, namely, the voluntary organization of public opinion and the invention of means of open propaganda, the objective being first to inform and persuade people about the facts of any given subject, and then by wake of an enlightened public opinion to bring pressure to bear upon the government of the day." This quotation from Lewis Waddilove's *One Man's Vision* suggests that the atmosphere in which Rowntree was brought up had considerable influence on how he approached philanthropy. He once wrote,

"The student of history soon finds that the arch-enemy of social progress is militarism; when this is in the ascendent, social reform is at a standstill. Perhaps no greater service could be rendered to the cause of human progress than to enter into the minds of the rising generation a hatred of war."

Arthur Sherwell, who worked with Joseph Rowntree in Temperance Reform, suggested that his breadth of comprehension, allied with and largely the fruit of a complete freedom from personal ambition, made him receptive to all suggestions and ideas from whatever source. None were rejected until they had been brought to the bar of a judgment whose balance was never deflected by personal predilection.

Accumulating years never imprisoned Rowntree in the ideas and opinions of the past. While his ideas about philanthropy remained consistent, his views on how best to bring about the social changes he sought were forever expanding. He never did approve of the benevolence that gave "thousands of pounds to build hospitals and sanitoriums." In his opinion, these things were the responsibility of the state and ought not to depend on private charity.[30] So, in addition to setting up a charitable trust, he set up a second trust to undertake social and political work that could not legally be supported by any funds belonging to a charitable trust. In essence the two trusts had the same purpose—to promote the general welfare. But while one was to meet public needs, the other was to change public attitudes and public policy.

Writing in *The Nation*, A. G. Gardiner suggested that there was in Rowntree an unusual fusion of the idealist and the realist, and his dreams were always kept within the firm grasp of an instructed and practical genius. He never grew old spiritually, and his mind remained fresh and accessible to new ideas to the end. Others who knew him argue that in all he touched his primary end was social service; he coveted business success first as a means of achieving that end.

PART THREE

The Quest for Meaning

INTRODUCTION

The Quest for Meaning

HUMANKIND HAS PAID A FRIGHTFUL PRICE for its obsession with things material, its preoccupation with what is considered practical, and its denial of the spiritual. As Harvey Cox wrote in *The Feast of Fools,* "Our emphasis on work, markets and community have sometimes enabled us to purchase prosperity at the staggering impoverishment of those vital elements like celebration and imagination that enable us to relate to the past and the future in ways that are impossible for other members of our species."[1]

The acts of generosity we celebrate are more likely to be those in which private beneficence healed the sick, found the cure for dreaded disease, or expanded educational opportunities. Yet, benevolent wealth has also been used to open up new cultural vistas, to extend the frontiers of knowledge, and to transform or transcend old absolutes. With the coming of industrialization, the great benefactors grew more sober and industrious—quite correctly responding to the social priorities of the time. But what of the spiritual dimension that lay outside the domain of the priests and prophets of organized religion?

In the revolutionary environment of Armenian life in the late Nineteenth and early Twentieth Centuries, the emphasis was on either the struggle for an independent Armenia or the support of Armenian refugees who were fleeing genocide at the hands of the Turks. But during the worst of the strife, and at almost the eye of the storm,

95

Calouste Gulbenkian, a wealthy Armenian, used a significant portion
of his wealth to acquire art objects of unusual value and significance.
He donated over 3,000 pieces to the Gulbenkian Foundation at his
death.

Some years later, when the Jews were returning to the land of
their ancestors to build a new Jerusalem—struggling against all con-
ceivable odds, from a harsh natural environment to violent opposition—Polly van Leer was using her wealth in Israel to search for
metaphysical answers. She brought to the shores of the Mediterranean a constant stream of thinkers and creative people, exploring what
her son Wim van Leer described as the "tortuous pathways of revealed
truth." She was in many ways a mystic, while many of her
contemporaries were militants, but they shared in common the search
for radically different answers to life as they had come to know
it.

In *The Myth of the Machine,* Lewis Mumford argued that we
have become so fascinated with early man as toolmaker we have
forgotten that before he made tools he made myths and rituals.[2]
This tendency to ignore the impact of the quest for meaning on
human activity has sometimes led to the labeling of those who bankroll
this search as eccentric and odd. Polly van Leer, in her unusual obsessions, and Calouste Gulbenkian, in his efforts to both affirm and
transcend his Armenian identity, were both possessed with a burning desire for a better future. They reflected in their philanthropy
Albert Camus' injunction in *The Rebel:* "The procedure of beauty,
which is to contest reality while endowing it with unity, is also
the procedure of rebellion.... History may perhaps have an end;
but our task is not to terminate it, but to create it."[3]

Both Calouste Gulbenkian and Polly van Leer provided in their
philanthropy a way to escape the limits of existing paradigms and
to create a new way of envisioning reality. They opened the door
to a "metaphysical rebellion" that was an affirmation of history
and a brief recess from history. In their lives and philanthropy, both
reality and fantasy commingled.

9

Calouste Gulbenkian
Turkey

THE ARMENIAN EMPIRE once extended from the Caspian Sea to the Mediterranean Sea. The first nation to officially accept Christianity, most Armenians take deep pride in their history, culture, and national church. But when they come together to reminisce, to dream, or to worship, they tell the story of how 1.8 million Armenians were murdered and more than one million more made refugees. Fleeing to any country that would take them, they lived in orphanages throughout childhood and then emigrated to Armenia to retrieve their families and to make meaningful lives for themselves. The Turkish campaign to wipe out the Armenians began in 1894 and reached its peak during World War I.

It was during these turbulent years of the late Nineteenth and early Twentieth Centuries that Calouste Gulbenkian came to occupy center stage in the Armenian drama. Born in Istanbul in 1869, he became a legendary oil financier and fabled art collector. By the time of his death in 1955, his annual income was reported to be in excess of $14 million, and his estate was valued at $420 million. A philanthropist who gave to myriad causes, he was also chairman of the Armenian General Benevolent Union. But while he is greatly honored and revered in Portugal and England, where the benefactions from his legacies continue, there are also critics who claim that he let his countrymen down in their hour of greatest need. Some deeply resented his generosity in support of the arts while Armenians were waging a desperate struggle for their existence as a people. Others wanted him to put his prestige and his money behind the struggle for an independent Armenia.

Gulbenkian's huge investments in art did not prohibit him from responding to humanitarian appeals, providing both charitable support and personal leadership in support of the cause of the refugees. But there was no way to ease the disappointment some felt regarding his position on an independent Armenia. According to his son Nubar, "He didn't believe in an independent Armenia at any time in his life.... He considered Armenian talents best adapted to making a livelihood and carving out a position in the world at large." One of his biographers suggested that if Gulbenkian had been a Jew, he would not have been a Zionist, wanting a state of Israel, but would have remained an "assimilator."[4]

This is the stuff from which both strong resentment and deep respect grow. Gulbenkian's name continues to engender both reactions. His passion for obscurity did not help matters. He was, to many, a mystery man. His fear of assassination, a paranoia developed while he was still young, kept him away from crowds and most public places. His sister-in-law described him as a man who "hated parties and people en-masse," but his son Nubar's comment was classic. He said that, "Father hated people, it's true, but he never hated an individual." Yet, this is the man who is credited in Lisbon and London with great foresight and charitable instinct in endowing a Portugese-based trust that has spread its activities to Iraq and other countries of the Middle East, to the Armenian communities throughout the world, and to the United Kingdom.

—————

The fashioning of the Gulbenkian legacy began with Calouste's father, a petroleum importer who was one of the Turkish pioneers in obtaining kerosene under contract to sell it to the Sultan and his dictatorship in Europe and Asia. He also founded a merchant banking house that lent money and financed businesses throughout the Ottoman Empire. For generations, the Gulbenkians had been in-termarrying: Armenian communities were not only scarce in Asia Minor, but they sought to maintain their distinct racial and religious characteristics and their close ties in the face of persecution. They were also responding to an urge to keep money and other possessions in the family. Perhaps as a result of the inbreeding, the first Gulbenkian child died in infancy. The second, Calouste, was a child prodigy.

Not much is known about Calouste's mother, Dirouhe, except that she shared with his father the Armenian passion for education. While the Gulbenkians engaged English and French tutors for their children, they spoke only Armenian in the home. Like others in their time, they used the Armenian tongue to stir pride in the historic achievements of the race and to inculcate Christian values, with a special emphasis on thrift.

The elder Gulbenkian provided his son a good education, first at a modern American school in Constantinople, and later at Kings College in London, where he earned a degree in civil engineering. Matriculation at the American school was by selection and carried considerable prestige. It put young Calouste in contact with the sons of leading Turkish families. His thesis at Kings College was on mining engineering with particular reference to the petroleum industry. In 1892, while still in England, he married the daughter of another wealthy Armenian family, culminating a courtship that had started in 1887.

Calouste Gulbenkian returned home to enter his father's oil business and at the age of twenty-two published a highly technical report on what he had seen and learned while visiting the oil fields in Baku. His observations brought him to the attention of officials in the Ottoman government who asked him to draw up a report on the oil fields in Mesopotamia (now called Iraq). A pioneer in the development of oil in the Middle East, he was far ahead of his time in anticipating the need and potential for an international oil industry.

The complexity of Gulbenkian's personality—with a concomitant ambiguity in values—began to surface. Having been brought up in a patriarchal society, he became, as he grew older, a dictator in family matters, but he was unable to fully subdue his wife Nevarte. She had wit, vitality, and charm, and she provided the family with a cultured and civilized atmosphere. Her sister, Atvarte Essayon, described her as providing a social background for Calouste that was of the utmost importance to his career. However, the Gulbenkian's son, Nubar, reported that while his mother came from a moneyed background, after marriage (typical of her time) she never had any money that she could call her own. If she wanted cars, furs, or jewels she had first to ask her husband. Nubar saw this as a kind of invidious submission.

There was also the matter of Nevarte's dowry. Calouste and his two brothers were given £30,000 by their father. While still young, they went into the carpet business together and lost all their money. Calouste then took his wife's dowry—which was legally his, but even under the Victorian Code she still had some ethical claims to it. He used it partly to extract a Mesopotamian oil concession from the Turks, but he refused to help his brothers. His stated reason for not coming to their aid was that he did not believe "in throwing good money after bad," but others accused him of calculating that the disaster would disgrace his two brothers in their father's eyes and improve his own chances of benefiting from his father's will.

The concern about the use of the dowry remained. Just before her death, Nevarte wrote a letter instructing that this money be used for the development and endowment of an Armenian orphanage. Calouste's failure to provide for the orphanage led to tensions between him and his son that lasted until his own will was drawn up ten years later.

Meanwhile, the economic and political environment was drawing Calouste Gulbenkian into a revelation of the full measure of his moral character and charitable instincts. An international oil industry was beginning to take shape, and Calouste performed a very important role in the organization of the Royal Dutch–Shell Group. He was also a link between the American and Russian oil industries and, in fact, gave the first boost to this industry in the Persian Gulf. But on the political side, his fellow Armenians found their very existence threatened. By 1877, when Turkey lost its war against Russia, Armenian hopes for independence had reached a new crescendo. But in 1894, the Turks began a campaign to exterminate the Armenians. It was a deadly escalation of a conflict that had begun in 1514, when the Ottoman Turks first gained control of Armenia. (Many, most prominent among them the Turkish government, do not agree that the massacre of Armenians was the result of a systematic policy of the Ottoman Empire.)

This was a time of intense grief for Armenians. Commemorating the tragedy many years later, Professor Richard Hovannisian of the University of California at Los Angeles described the Armenian legacy as not just a culture of art, music, literature, and language, but the trauma of an unacknowledged genocide. At a National Gathering of Survivors, a meeting in Washington, D.C., in 1985, Nevarte Paraseghian Hagopian, a 76-year-old woman from Granite City, Illinois, described her experience in Moush, Turkey. "They brought all the young men of the village, all chained, to a barn," she recalled in tentative English. "There were 500, 600. I was six years old. We went to take water to them. They wanted cigarettes, so we got them cigarettes. And matches. Then a Turk threw me out of the barn. And they started the barn on fire. The noise of that is still in my ear."[5]

To avoid massacre, the Gulbenkians fled to Egypt, where they found refuge with Nubar Pasha, a man to whom Calouste was related by marriage. An Armenian who served as one of the leaders of Egypt for twenty years (as foreign minister or president of the Khedive's Council of Ministers), Pasha was involved in the Suez Canal Project. The family connection gave Gulbenkian a new status. He was friend, protégé and "nephew" of the world-famous statesman and was introduced to the financial advisor of the Prince of Wales, and to leaders of French diplomacy and finance, including the Rothschilds. He soon made other important friends and gained entrée into the highest diplomatic and financial circles in Western Europe.

As his international connections enhanced his international stature, Calouste became a naturalized British citizen. He was thus assured of the protection of a great Western power. Meanwhile, he maintained a foot in the Oriental camp, serving as financial advisor to the Turks.

He had a house in Bayswater and another in Paris, as well as permanent suites at the Ritz in both London and Paris. His work did not involve an office routine, so he rarely was to be found at the Turkish Petroleum Company (later the Iraq Oil Company) he created. His best thinking was done on walks: he took morning walks in Hyde Park and visited art galleries or antique shops in the afternoon. After dinner, he was usually on the telephone until midnight. A health faddist, he lived for a time on a massive diet of carrots and turnip juice.

Ralph Hewins composed an imaginary "Who's Who" entry describing Gulbenkian as a financier, industrialist, diplomat, churchman, philanthropist, connoisseur, and Casanova.[6] Stories about his mistresses abound, but he was, in his way, a family man. He and his wife had two children, a son, Nubar (born in 1896) and a daughter, Rita (born in 1900). Nubar was essentially disinherited. He was a playboy who had several wives and innumerable "female friends." He wore an orchid in his lapel every day, wrote his autobiography, and made no apparent contribution to the events of his time. Rita married a cousin in a family-arranged marriage and had one son.

Calouste's relationship to his wife Nevarte was one of a series of contradictions. She kept the family together despite the claims that he had a new mistress every year until he was eighty. If this was true, then the Gulbenkians must have had a practical understanding. Ralph Hewins wrote that, "In his peculiar way he loved her as he loved nobody else. To him, she was both a good wife and an asset. She had become part of his routine, a habit, a fixture. . . . She ran his homes with charm and efficiency and had the wisdom to take his peccadillos for what they were, shallow distractions."[7]

Gulbenkian was under various forms of pressure for years, battling single-handedly for his rights with the great powers and big oil combines. He did business with both British and Russian interests, worked with the French in the founding of their oil production industry and organized the American entry into the Turkish Petroleum Company, thus shaping Middle East oil development for many years. But his great love and legacy was art. By shrewd trading and dogged determination, he acquired one of the finest private collections in the world. His holdings ranged from Rembrandts and Rubenses to the works of Renoir and Monet and the famed *September Morn* of Paul Chabas. His interest in art was expansive, including not only painting but Egyptian sculpture, Oriental ceramics, manuscripts, old books and bookbindings, and objects of Syrian glass, French furniture, tapestry and textiles, Lalique jewelry, and Greek antiquities. One of his most significant acquisitions was the purchase of the original marble statue of the famous Diana, by Houdon, which belonged to Catherine of Russia and which he bought from the Hermitage in Leningrad in 1930.

Although he was tight-fisted with his family, Gulbenkian was involved in considerable acts of generosity. He was a major benefactor of the Armenian Patriarchate of Jerusalem, to which he donated a library. Like his Armenian peers, he was a devout worshipper in the Armenian Church: he built the Church of St. Sarkis in London and dedicated it to his parents. He was especially supportive of the Armenian communities and "fashioned an heir after his own heart—the Calouste Gulbenkian Foundation." In accordance with the terms of his will, the purposes of the foundation were to be charitable, artistic, educational, and scientific. While an international citizen with homes and contacts in several countries, he found a peace and pace in Portugal that he came to revere. So he chose this country, which he had not entered until the Second World War, as the headquarters for his new philanthropic trust.

Gulbenkian's will also made important bequests to his children and provided life pensions for the benefit of other family members and persons who had assisted him for many years. In 1976, on the twentieth anniversary of the establishment of the Calouste Gulbenkian Foundation, the trustees and other notables paid tribute to the Gulbenkian largesse. He was hailed for his "creative genius and often exhausting work" which culminated to "the advantage of humanity in the form of material and spiritual benefits." The statement of the occasion declared, "The way in which Calouste Gulbenkian used his fortune during his active lifetime and the use to which the estate was put after his death, was typical of his perfect understanding of the social function of wealth and the moral obligation of the wealthy."

A private man who deliberately sought anonymity, there are still many people who remain unaware of the altruistic ideas that had inspired him for some time. What were those ideas? Were Gulbenkian's values and motivations somehow overlooked by his critics? Those who now carry out his legacy seek to answer those questions.

We have already seen that Gulbenkian's notion of cultural pluralism got him into trouble with some of his contemporaries. He saw his destiny in larger terms than implied in his Armenian identity and the limits some placed on community obligation. He was a realist who felt, especially after the death and dispersal of so many Armenians, that there were not enough people left to form a workable, free Armenian state. His concern and his compassion for his community were reflected in his work as chairman of the Armenian General Benevolent Union. Not only was he a generous contributor himself, but he raised money from his friends as well. Avetoom P. Hacobian, who was one of Gulbenkian's chief aides in his philanthropic endeavors, described his benefactions in these words: "All his life, including the Second World War, and afterwards, Mr. Gulbenkian sent great benefactions to Armenian charities everywhere—to almost every country in the world, including the countries behind the Iron Curtain. The Treasury made special arrangements for him to transfer the necessary currency. It was a great labor keeping up with his wishes and the files on this one branch of his activity became enormous."[8]

There was a tradition among the wealthy Armenians that they should leave as much as nine-tenths of their money to Armenian charity. But Gulbenkian left almost his entire fortune and all his possessions to the Gulbenkian Foundation. That was what irritated some of his critics. The magnitude of his investment in art—he owned over 3,000 items—was another sticky point. Whereas his contributions to the Armenian refugee cause and his other activities in behalf of his community were humanitarian in their intent, it was in the other uses of his wealth that he was accused of excessive self-indulgence. Yet his contributions of art may be his greatest legacy. The Gulbenkian Museum in Lisbon, a specially constructed building that houses his entire collection, is now considered one of the best museums of decorative art in existence.

The conflict between material and spiritual benefit is a natural tension in a revolutionary environment. Yet both are needed to create that essential wholeness that can provide the capacity for self-assertion and dignity. Thus Gulbenkian's interest in the arts was bound to lead to different reactions from a people fighting not only for their humanity and freedom, but for their survival. Even today, Armenians argue vigorously over public tactics and private largesse; some support such groups as the Secret Army for the Liberation of Armenia, whereas others strongly object to the tactics of the Secret Army against Turkish diplomats and other targets of their frustration and anger.

While Calouste Gulbenkian's full motives and values may never be clear, there is little doubt that he was a deeply religious man. The national church has been and continues to be at the center of Armenian life. In the minds of many people, it is the church that makes an Armenian an Armenian. Gulbenkian was no different from his peers in this regard. He was a devout worshipper and strong supporter of Armenian religious traditions. But the great attractiveness of Gulbenkian, and the momentous legacy of his life, is the reminder that in the passion to create a new human future, many people overlook the need to focus on and foster culture, to provide outlets for creativity and imagination, to prepare the way for a regeneration of the spirit. His motives may have been both noble and self-indulgent, but his struggle to respond to both the humanitarian appeals of his fellow Armenians and the need for moments of transcendence reflects the essential dualism of human nature. Moreover, even the most generous acts in behalf of others are sometimes driven by the quest for meaning in the life of the benefactor.

10

Polly van Leer
Israel

POLLY VAN LEER USED HER WEALTH in search of a larger meaning for herself and her community. She was a Jew, committed to the idea of a homeland with a special national calling and destiny, but her sense of belonging transcended national boundaries. Revered by some of her colleagues for her support of scholars and scientists, she was ridiculed by others for her disturbing obsessions. Her legacy, the van Leer Jerusalem Foundation, is now one of the most important philanthropic institutions in Israel. Likewise, the building she designed and donated is now an important center of intellectual inquiry and new thinking.

Many people who knew Polly van Leer would argue that she was not a philanthropist and does not belong in this volume. She is, however, the perfect example of a donor who came to be more highly regarded after her death than in her lifetime. This contradiction was underscored by one acquaintance who said, "I don't consider her a philanthropist; she was more of a self-indulgent pain who used her money to force her attention on prominent people for her own selfish purposes. And whatever good might come from the Jerusalem Foundation had little to do with her. It was rescued from ridicule by those who picked up the pieces."

What were Polly van Leer's motives? Was her quest for meaning outside the boundaries of the other-serving values generally reflected in philanthropy? It is true that she did not have a sustained history of charitable contributions and was not involved in conventional forms of benevolence, but she used her private wealth for public purposes while seeking no material gain. Her motives and her methods are not without contradictions, but she is not alone in this regard; the idiosyncracies of some of the world's most celebrated philanthropists are legend.

Jerusalem was a perfect setting for Polly van Leer. Here, in the shadow of the Tower of David and its reminders of past glory, stands the building she designed as a monument to the future. Described by some as "Polly's folly," it is the center not only of long-standing controversy but also of continuing curiosity. This is only fitting, for in the life and philanthropy of Polly van Leer we find introspection raised to the level of ritual and the charitable impulse a human paradox. In Polly van Leer there was a kind of intellectual thrashing about in search of bits of wisdom—a fascination with intellectual fragments but little tolerance for metaphysical systems or fully developed answers.

To some, this seemed like an indulgence—even anti-intellectual— but this woman, who was largely self-educated, was persistent in her search for a higher reason. She could not accept the neat little boxes, political or ideological, that divided people into "we" and "they" groups. She wanted to build a new community in which members provided mutual support in their efforts to transcend religious bigotry and obsessive nationalism.

Her other preoccupation, no less visionary, was the establishment of a new Jerusalem and, by extension, a radically different world. She talked long and searched widely for ideas that would help recruit others to her obsession. While this utopian phase of her life tells us little about her experience as a wife, a mother, or the daughter of a pillar of the Jewish community in Amsterdam, it does provide a perspective on the passion that drove her for most of her years in Jerusalem.

Her two sons were on their own: Oscar was making his way as an entrepreneur and Wim was pursuing his own fascinations. Meanwhile her husband, Bernard, was traveling from one capital to another, firmly securing and expanding the van Leer business enterprises. There seemed to be little family affection or even social interaction, but Polly was plowing her own ground in the fertile soil of her ancestors.

Bernard, whom she married in 1912, was an industrialist who survived a Nazi takeover of his factories to rebuild his far-flung financial empire. The Hague-based Bernard van Leer Foundation his son Oscar created in his father's name is distinguished both by its ownership of a thriving business enterprise and by the practice of awarding more than 90 percent of its grants outside of its home base in Holland. Moreover, its support of the developmental needs of children in more than thirty countries has gained it a reputation as one of the most important foundations in Europe.

Bernard van Leer was the prototype of the educated young man who, through hard work and dedication, achieved economic success and international stature. He dined with heads of state and somehow even persuaded the Germans during the Nazi occupation to let him, his family, and his horses slip quietly out of Holland to relocate in the United States. His story and his successes represent the kind of accomplishments the world celebrates and honors.

Some would say it was absurd for Polly van Leer, with her theories and incessant questioning, to assume that she was qualified to develop a blueprint for a better world. But if this wealthy woman seemed confused—and certainly odd—to the scholars she summoned to Jerusalem, it was because she was desperately trying to hammer out a philosophy that might contribute to the development of a more humane society. She was in many ways a product of her time. There was a special aura of transcendence on the eastern shores of the Mediterranean Sea as Jews from all parts of the world came together to build what idealists among them described as a more perfect human society. They refused to yield to conventional wisdom or to be bound by social, political, or economic limits. Like her fellow visionaries, Polly van Leer felt free to dream the impossible dream. But while others were draining swamps, irrigating deserts, planting forests, restoring mountains, and building a Jewish state, Polly was dreaming of the spiritual rebirth of a people, an intellectual renaissance of the mind, and a moral reaffirmation of ancient truths.

Polly was born in the Netherlands in 1896 to well-to-do Dutch parents. Her father was administrator of the local Jewish Religious Council in Amsterdam, where he also had a seat on the Stock Exchange. As the official dispenser of the Jewish community's charities, he introduced Polly at an early age to the needs of the poor, the unemployed, and those living on the margins of Dutch society. Yet as she grew older, she embarked on an almost endless search for a higher form of benevolence. She was not interested in charity, but in the development of the full potential of the individual.

While Polly van Leer would be the first to deny that she ever achieved her ideal, there is no denying that she set out to create a new understanding of civic obligation. Her commitment, passion, and contradictions are all reflected in the institutions she fashioned.

She asked the deeper questions of meaning and purpose. She was concerned with moral values and with how each individual might contribute to building a better world. But Polly van Leer also left her contemporaries perplexed by her unwillingness to settle down to a life of ease and luxury. Her restlessness with dogma and the closed minds of renowned scholars and statesmen led her to become an unforgettable iconoclast. Shy and retiring in some ways, bold and imaginative in others, Polly van Leer was eccentric and colorful enough to gain a hearing among the most powerful and the most learned people of her time.

Deeply concerned with the holocaust—Why did the six million have to die? Was there a purpose, an idea, a future behind it?— Polly van Leer felt her Jewishness with a special passion. Yet she wrote that, in essence, humankind through all the ages has been concerned with the same problems, and the self-imposed obligation to solve them remains the same. Humankind must bring peace to the world—justice and liberty to all individual groups.[9]

She believed, with the historian Tacitus, that patriotism was a kind of competition with one's ancestors, and that each generation must build upon the achievements of the previous generation by contributing to all that has been achieved before. It is not surprising that she agonized over the question, "what can be the contribution of our time?"

On June 23, 1973, the day after Polly van Leer died, a small group of her friends, closely associated with the work of the van Leer Jerusalem Foundation, met to reflect on the themes central to her thought and closest to her heart. Yehuda Elkana, who was selected to give concreteness and reality to the emotional and intellectual focus of Polly van Leer's life, wrote:

> She was deeply interested in the meaning of religion, yet herself was secular and abhorred religious fanaticism and dogma. She cared very little for the external symbols of any religion. Not the candles, the paraphernalia, the "Kipah" or the dietary laws for her. But neither was it the Christian emphasis on the artistic–spiritual accompaniment of religion, like music or sculpture that interested her. It was the pure dematerialized "idea" and the essence of things that mattered to her. In this she was unmistakably of the thousand-years-old family of Jewish intellectuals.[10]

How did this Dutch woman, who experienced both the Nazi occupation of Holland and an unremarkable sojourn in the United States, come to be honored at 43 Jabotinsky Street in Jerusalem, next door to the residence of the President of Israel? Those who knew her tell fascinating stories about her determination, her romance with ideas, her quest for unity. She was concerned with two problems: universal unity and Jewish survival. Deeply committed to the belief that "out of Zion shall come forth the light," she was far from an extreme nationalist. The light that was to come out of Zion should not only serve all the people, all the religions of the world, the rich and poor alike, but it should also be jointly produced by all nations of all faiths.[11]

Polly van Leer came to believe that civilization is primarily concentrated upon the accumulation of knowledge and its technical applications, whereas human beings, in the true sense of their humanity,
are left behind. She wanted, therefore, to contribute to a change
in the mental attitude of humankind. The way she set out to do
it reveals as much about her values and motivations as it does about
her approach to philanthropy. The van Leer Jerusalem Foundation
building she erected in Jerusalem was, for her, at least symbolically,
the "Third Temple." The architects and others who worked with
her regarded their experience as a nightmare, but no one can enter
the magnificent structure without realizing that something extraordinary is being portrayed. Built on the most expensive real estate
in Jerusalem, with a funnel-shaped ceiling pointing to the heavens
and an imposing library, auditorium, and conference rooms peopled
with scholars, it reflects both the audacity and tenacity of its donor.
Because Jerusalem was holy to three great religions, Polly van Leer
felt that the whole of Israel should have symbolized the Third Temple.
Yehuda Elkana described this conception of a Third Temple as a
passion that drove her again and again toward the rabbis, priests,
and pastors, but she came up each time against the forbidding walls
of dogma. Less than satisfied with the answers of Judaism, Christianity,
and Islam, she wanted to travel to the Far East to continue her
search for the meaning of the human predicament, but she never
lived to do so.

How could a person be so abstract and secular while at the same
time so committed to the basic values of equality and human potential?
Seymour Fox, a professor at the Hebrew University of Jerusalem,
described his first meeting with Polly van Leer in 1956: "She was
a very gracious hostess and made me feel very comfortable, but she
pressed her questions on me to the point that I left her home impressed
but tired." At a second meeting, she began the conversation by pointing
to a map of the Middle East and saying, "We are a small country
surrounded by millions of Arabs who want to destroy us. To continue
to exist under these conditions requires that we have a clear conception
of our convictions, and those convictions must be on the highest
moral plain."

She went on to ask Professor Fox what convictions he wanted young people in Israel to adopt. In the course of the conversation, he was struck by what he described as her overwhelming passion for "unity between science and religion, unity between men, between cultures and nations." Yehuda Elkana, who has taught at Harvard and Brandeis and at the Hebrew University of Jerusalem, said that there was scarcely a great physicist, molecular biologist, or evolutionary expert who was not approached by Polly van Leer at some stage in her search and confronted with the question, "What are the lessons of science for man?" She was not, however, interested in science for the sake of science. She wanted science and scientists to do something about the world's ills. She wanted research to take place against the backdrop of values. The more she sought out and got to know the great scholars and humanists of her time, the more she came to realize their limitations. Her obstinate single-mindedness nearly drove her associates mad, but she was a friend of David Ben-Gurion and the many idealists who sought to make Israel a new society based on higher values. "We cannot hope to arrive at a fundamental change by approaching, or even solving, any one of the problems which confront us," she warned. "We must go deeper and penetrate into and concentrate fully on the very heart and source of man's doing, his thinking."

Calling for a new phase in man's development, she argued that this change must take place in people's minds. Polly van Leer had the incessant urge to put the essence of her thoughts into some form of coherent philosophy, but she concluded that instead of trying to provide a working program, she would describe a point of departure. She borrowed ideas; she refined and frequently redefined them, but she finally put together a little booklet that she described as embodying the thoughts of a lifetime. Not surprisingly, she called it "The Point of Departure."

Writing about his mother many years later, Wim van Leer referred to her "philosophical flavor of the week," reflecting the many turns her thoughts took on the road to coherence and clarity. Her quest for "reason and meaning" in her spiritual home, Jerusalem, seemed so far from the Holland of her youth, where she had paid weekly

visits to Amsterdam's colorful ghetto to distribute her largesse among
the poor and needy. While there is some question about what she
read and even more about what she understood, she filled her shelves
with the works of Martin Buber and other popular philosophers.
Her library also included the Bible and other works upon which
she built a metaphysical structure that served as the basis for the
arguments she initiated and pursued with dogged determination.

Her personal philosophy, or better yet, her *search* for a personal
philosophy, began to take shape in the years of the Nazi occupation
of Holland. Yet it was after her return from the United States, while
her husband was building his industrial group, that she really began
to take an interest in the many orthodoxies of her time. She was
first fascinated by the thoughts of Geradus Bolland, a Dutch philosopher who was so celebrated that a learned society was established
to distribute his thoughts. But she found only temporary satisfaction
in his works and later turned to the ideas of Hegel. This flirtation
with ideas brought to the van Leers many of the learned people
of the time. One by one they were discarded—often after some cookies
and Scotch—and others brought in for a ride on Polly's intellectual hobbyhorse.

Probably few incidents describe the woman who seemed so restless
with her own intellectual paradigms better than a symposium she
hosted in Jerusalem. She invited a large number of scholars and learned
thinkers to an all-expenses-paid discussion—which broke up almost
as soon as it started; another group of sages had been identified,
lectured on her brand of metaphysics, and sent packing. For a woman
who left school at the age of twelve, she had a surprising appetite
for ideas. It was clear, however, that she had little time for humility,
for she lectured more than she listened.

Polly van Leer's philanthropic dream was to build an Israeli Academy
of Sciences of great prestige, and an institute to attract and house
the best minds in the world. Her vision still guides the van Leer
Jerusalem Foundation, created in 1956. It is presently involved in
a wide variety of efforts to improve relations between Arabs and
Jews, to understand the conflicts and coherence between science and

human values, and to harmonize one's personal obligation to society with his/her right to realize inborn potential.

Polly's quest for a higher reason was also a search for a more perfect form of philanthropy. She left a legacy that differs radically from the charitable activities of her father and those of the Bernard van Leer Foundation named after her husband. As she was motivated by her own brand of metaphysics, it is only fitting that the foundation she created is housed in a building that stands as a monument to the complexity of her vision.

Deeply committed to human equality, she was first and foremost the servant of ideas. According to Yehuda Elkana, who now directs the foundation, her egalitarian spirit worked both ways, "equal respect for the humble and the poor, but no reverence or concession for the mighty and important." The little Dutch girl transformed her father's interest in charity and the news of the day into her very special kind of philanthropy. As Eric Kahlerl, the great historian, wrote in reference to her aims and ambitions, "The task of rescuing human culture from threatening decay is enormous." But who is to judge whether Polly van Leer's use of her wealth was good philanthropy, or even relevant? She blazed a new trail in demonstrating that wealth used for public purposes need not be a traditional form of public beneficence, nor the support of dull ideas or accepted orthodoxies. The work her foundation is now doing to prevent chauvinism and particularism; to lessen tensions between people who differ in culture, religion, political views, and dogma; and to call attention to the moral uses of knowledge is a monument to the woman who was as disturbing as she was disturbed, who used private wealth to "afflict the comfortable rather than simply comfort the afflicted."

Polly van Leer died disappointed and bitter about her inability to persuade and enlist others to her point of view. She finally came to believe that the world was not ready for her vision. But Fred Simon, her first administrator, who had come from America to help build a new Jerusalem, saw in her work the potential for a new way of thinking and being. There is no doubt that her refusal to accept absolutes—her tireless questioning of what others regarded as profound—could serve her beloved Jerusalem well in the present struggle among competing orthodoxies. Israel's sense of identity is troubled these days by the very fissures in the community that Polly van Leer anticipated and struggled to prevent.

PART FOUR

Mixed Motives, or Tainted Generosity

INTRODUCTION

Mixed Motives, or Tainted Generosity

BERNARD MANDEVILLE, an Eighteenth Century English critic, sought to expose what he regarded as the hypocrisy underlying the motives of the philanthropists of his time. In his book, *Fable of the Bees*, subtitled "Private Vices, Public Benefits," he attributed private beneficence as much to fear, vanity, and pride as to moral injunctions and civic virtue. Mandeville's mentor, La Rochefoucauld, once observed, "We often do good, in order that we may do evil with impunity." But is the charitable act that results in a better life for a fellow citizen any less meaningful or desirable because of the motives of the giver?

Ryoichi Sasakawa, a Japanese philanthropist who presides over motorboat racing and the gambling associated with the sport, has been described as a gambling czar, rightist agitator, political power broker, and suspected war criminal. He is also alleged to have close ties with the Unification Church, a religious group whose leader, Sun Myung Moon, was jailed in the United States for fraud. Some Japanese are openly displeased with both the source of his generosity and the public attention that surrounds his philanthropy. Critics in England staged a public protest against his participation in efforts to bail out an international sports venture, claiming that his money was tainted.

Adnan Khashoggi, once referred to as the richest man in the world, was a prime subject of the United States Senate Subcommittee on Multinational Corporations investigation of international bribery.

Flamboyant and a middleman with a leading role in a variety of international business deals, Khashoggi's name was one of the first to surface in the highly publicized arms-for-hostages deal with Iran that embarrassed and crippled the Reagan presidency.

Critics accuse Sasakawa of seeking to buy the Nobel Peace Prize he so highly covets, and Khashoggi of using philanthropy as a public relations tool to improve his image. But for the black students at Morehouse College in Atlanta, Georgia, who have benefited from Sasakawa's largesse, and the trustees of American University in Washington, D.C., who elected Khashoggi to their board, there seems to be more interest in the benefits of philanthropy than in the motives of the benefactor.

For those whose lives are relieved from social distress or to whom happiness is given, the charitable act is often meritorious regardless of its motive. The two men profiled in this section have known their share of controversy. But while their motives may be mixed, or their money tainted, as their critics claim, their life stories are punctuated with tales of good deeds.

11

Adnan Mohamed Khashoggi
Saudi Arabia

ADNAN MOHAMED KHASHOGGI was once considered the richest man in the world. A product of the new wealth in the Middle East, he contributed to society by creating jobs and donating money. Even some of his business dealings were regarded as having altruistic purposes. But he is best known for his flamboyance, his extravagant life-style, his high commissions from U.S. corporations (some called them bribes), and his role in questionable arms deals. While much less is known about his benevolence, he has also made sizable donations to charitable causes.

When he pledged a $5 million contribution for a $14 million sports complex at American University in Washington, D.C., Khashoggi was doing what his fellow trustees expected and what the university president had hoped. But some students protested and urged the university to reject his largesse. It did not matter that they badly needed the facility. The student protestors (and some faculty) objected to the way in which Khashoggi made his money, particularly his highly publicized role as the middleman in the arms-for-hostages deal that badly tarnished the Reagan presidency.

The Eagle, the student newspaper at American University, devoted considerable space to Khashoggi's pledge, including a stinging commentary by its editorial page editor, who wondered whether the university considered moral implications when making decisions about the appointment of trustees or the acceptance of gifts. She wrote that the university was "so enthralled at the prospect of having a sports center that we neglected to really look at who was donating the money and who was to carry the name. It was a mistake to knowingly have on our board of trustees a world famous (and infamous) arms dealer; it was an even greater mistake to accept his gratuity."[1]

Was it a mistake? Another student, writing in the same issue of *The Eagle,* argued that "idealism can only go so far. We need this center. . . . Until Khashoggi came along with his big bucks, a sports center on the AU campus was nothing more than a distant dream."[2] While some students raised moral questions, American University president Richard Berendzen downplayed the issue. When *The Washington Post* reported that the campus was in the throes of a debate, Berendzen disagreed, calling the report "a totally misleading and hyped-up story." He acknowledged that Khashoggi was a controversial figure, but he argued that over the last hundred years many of the major philanthropists we now honor were also controversial in their time. He specifically singled out Cornelius Vanderbilt, for whom Vanderbilt University is named, as a man who was "not just controversial, but a man who had significant legal problems."

Berendzen thus refused to accept the allegation that the largesse of his wealthiest trustee was tainted. Putting Khashoggi in some highly vener- ated company, Berendzen is quoted by Ronald Kessler in *The Richest Man in the World* as saying, "So are President Reagan and Jesus Christ" controversial. He went on to remind his critics that even the money for the highly esteemed Nobel Prize came from an inventor of dynamite. "Is Khashoggi any more controversial than Alfred Nobel?" Berendzen asked.[3]

The presidents of Haverford and Swarthmore colleges in Pennsyl- vania had responded very differently a few years earlier. They had been invited to apply to Khashoggi's newly created Triad Foundation for scholarship funds for students from the Middle East, for library funds, and for programs to hire professors. But when word of the application hit the college newspapers, local Jewish leaders expressed concern about both the source and the purpose of the benefaction. Both Haverford and Swarthmore withdrew their applications. Controversy in business deal- ings was nothing new to Adnan Khashoggi, but this was philanthropy.

Why should anyone reject the outright goodwill of an unencumbered benefaction?

To understand the objections to accepting Khashoggi's generosity, it is necessary to know more about the man who is reported to have been worth $2–4 billion at one time. His values and his wealth were both shaped by the experience of growing up in the early years of the newly established state of Saudi Arabia. Like Khashoggi's own life story, the young country was a land of considerable contrast. Nearly all desert, it is also a land of mysterious underground springs. While its inhabitants sleep at night in temperatures that sometimes drop to zero, they wander through 120-degree heat by day. Saudi culture and values were the product of this unique desert environment, as well as the religious practices of Islam.

Khashoggi was thus exposed to two dominant traditions of altruism. The first was the desert ethic of the Bedouin nomads, who had developed their own cultural mores and standards long before the Prophet Mohamed introduced a new religion. Their lives centered on the search for water for their cattle and their goats. Constantly on the move, the Bedouins developed a tradition of hospitality to the strangers they met as they traveled through endless miles of shifting sands. It was a desert ethic of survival, but it embraced the fellow traveler as well as family and friend without regard to religion or status. Their generosity was such that they not only abhorred the word *bakbil*, which meant "stingy one," but even their raids on other tribes were in accordance with a highly developed sense of morality and protocol. Camels could be taken, but lives were spared and women were inviolate.[4]

The second tradition of benevolence to which Khashoggi was exposed was the Islamic practice of collecting alms for the needy. The formal act was called *zakat*, a word derived from the Arab verb *zaka*, which means to be just, to be good and pure. Originally a voluntary practice, it evolved into a form of regulated tax.

Khashoggi was born into a family that had, for several generations, subscribed to the charitable ethic of Islam. His grandfather had served as mayor of Medina, one of the two cities (Mecca is the other) that occupy a special place in the hearts of Moslems. It was here that the Prophet Mohamed lived and preached and where the faithful believe that he received the Koran, the sacred book of Islam. Because Mecca and Medina are located in Saudi Arabia, the country continues to be the unofficial homeland of Islam, whose adherents not only give to the needy but also regard the act of giving as a pillar of their religion.

When at home in Saudi Arabia, Khashoggi can often be seen praying to Allah in the white *thobe* of his Arab ancestors. He is very familiar with the teachings of his religion regarding altruistic behavior, but he has added his own touch. In an interview in the January 19, 1987 issue of *Time* magazine, he made a distinction between compassion and realism. To emphasize the difference, he told the story of an oppressive summer afternoon when he discovered a beggar asleep on the front steps. He was only eight years old at the time, but knowing of Islam's emphasis on charity, he brought the man inside, gave him food, and invited him to sleep in the cool hall. Expecting great praise from his father for his compassion, he was surprised that when his father returned that evening he got a lecture instead. The young Khashoggi was told that while his intentions were good, he may have ruined the man's life, causing him never to be able to sleep on the sidewalk again.

Khashoggi used this incident to make the point that, "Compassion must be tempered with logic and logic with compassion." This is the philosophy of life by which he lives and it is the basic principle that undergirds his philanthropy. Private beneficence is, for him, more than an emotional response to a perceived need or a moving appeal; it is a rational, calculated act that seeks to accomplish a specific end.

It is not unusual for Khashoggi to turn to a boyhood experience with his father to explain his view of the social responsibility of wealth. His father was clearly the first major influence in his life. After graduation from the Sorbonne in Paris and medical school in Damascus, Syria, the elder Khashoggi became court physician to Abdul-Aziz, who had conquered the feuding tribes and sheikdoms and created the Kingdom of

Saudi Arabia. The two became very close friends, and Khashoggi often advised the King on matters far beyond the normal sphere that was formally the province of a private family doctor.

Adnan Khashoggi's gregarious and fun-loving personality seems to be a direct inheritance from his father, who entertained lavishly and was friendly and outgoing. Adnan, the eldest of six children, was born in Saudi Arabia in 1935, three years after Abdul-Aziz had proclaimed the country an Islamic monarchy. Young Adnan frequently accompanied his father to activities normally out of the reach of commoners (Saudis not·members of the royal family).

Khashoggi's early schooling was at a boarding school in Egypt. There, he met some of the future leaders of the Arab world, including the young Hussein, who later became King of Jordan. After graduating at the age of seventeen, Adnan spent three semesters at Chico State College and one semester at Stanford University in California. It was while he was in college that he sharpened his skills as a deal-maker. Having originally set out to become an engineer, he left school to become a full-time intermediary, a negotiator who served as a go-between for transacting parties.

The notion of intermediary is fundamental to the cultural and business practices of the Saudis. The concept emanates from the Islamic belief that in making his will known to Mohamed, God used Gabriel as an intermediary. The Arab word *wasta* literally means "go-between," a person who can vouch for both sides in a transaction. Khashoggi played this role with such zeal—he made hundreds of millions of dollars from U.S. businesses—that he very quickly came to the attention of the Senate Subcommittee on Multinational Corporations. That committee had been set up to look into allegations that U.S. companies had bribed foreign officials. Its chairman, Senator Frank Church, was determined to stop practices that he considered unfair, unethical, and corrupt.

The Idaho Democrat developed a passion for his work that angered many Wall Street power brokers and those who represented them. But he persevered, exposing practices that led the Securities and Exchange Commission to take action against many well-known companies. In addition, highly placed intermediaries in other countries, such as the former Japanese Prime Minister Kakuei Tanaka, were implicated.

The Church committee's investigation of Khashoggi lasted three years and involved trips to places of intrigue around the world. In the end, the staff accumulated massive amounts of information on Khashoggi's business dealings, including stories of alleged bribes and commissions amounting to tens of millions of dollars. These activities, coupled with other disclosures from U.S. companies, led to the enactment of the Foreign Corrupt Practices Act of 1977. The Act prohibited payments to foreign officials for the purpose of gaining a competitive advantage in a business deal. Payments to any person with knowledge that he or she might make such a payoff was also prohibited. While no formal charges were brought against Khashoggi, the allegations and innuendo continued long after the Senate Subcommittee closed shop and Senator Church turned to other business.

It was during the height of the revelations about Northrop Aircraft, 3M, and Gulf Oil, among other companies, that Edward K. Moss, Khashoggi's public affairs consultant in Washington, decided that Americans should know more about the other side of his client who was receiving so much negative publicity. In 1975 alone, Khashoggi appeared in 28 separate stories in the The New York Times. He was also the subject of a television special the same year by the National Broadcasting Company.

What concerned Moss was that the focus on Khashoggi's life-style and business deals, and his conspicuous consumption, overlooked his many acts of generosity and goodwill. Moreover, the Khashoggi largesse was disorganized. He was constantly besieged by people seeking money for various humanitarian purposes, and he frequently responded. His philanthropy was usually ad hoc; grants in Saudi Arabia were in the hundreds of thousands of dollars, while his charitable giving outside— sending students to U.S. colleges, for example—totaled as much as $500,000 a year. Yet, from the perspective of Moss's public relations experience, Khashoggi was getting no credit for his generosity. So Moss recommended that his client establish a foundation.

Establishing a foundation would gain Khashoggi no financial advantage: Saudi Arabia did not have an income tax and, as a Saudi citizen, he was exempt from U.S. personal income tax. But the public relations value could not be discounted, especially given the public innuendo about bribery and arms dealing. In addition, a foundation would provide an opportunity for more systematic and objective analysis of need and the opportunity to consider how best to ensure maximum impact.

On December 12, 1975, the Triad Foundation was established in Washington, D.C. with Moss as executive director and a newly appointed board of directors. In its first year of operations the foundation made about $700,000 in grants, including $30,000 for flood relief in Manila, the Philippines; $100,000 for a mosque in Beirut, Lebanon; $25,000 to the Arab Press Association; and $1,500 for the Mayor's Christmas Tree Fund in Nairobi, Kenya. The publicity from the flap with Haverford, Swarthmore, and, later, Bryn Mawr colleges, led the administrators to move the foundation to London, and its name was changed to the Khashoggi Foundation.

From then on, Khashoggi conducted his philanthropy with the same flair and public relations skill with which he conducted his business enterprises. In fact, they were often intertwined. When he announced plans for a $1 billion real estate project in Salt Lake City, Utah, for example, he also announced that, as part of the development, he would renovate a local landmark. He was careful to go to the heart of the symbolism and theology of his new Mormon friends. The local landmark, one of the most elegant mansions in the city, Devereaux House, was once owned by Joseph Young, a son of the founder of the Mormon Church.

Several years later, when Khashoggi announced additional plans for the Salt Lake City project, he also announced a $1.2 million donation to build an international educational center at the Latter Day Saints Hospital. For the occasion, he flew in friends and members of his family from all over the world. The new center was to be named in honor of his father, who had visited Utah in 1977.

Even in the conservative environment of Brigham Young's Mormon Church, Khashoggi's largesse was accepted and blessed without question. A lavish dinner at Devereaux House was attended by Utah Governor Scott M. Matheson, as well as the acting president of the Mormon Church, Gordon P. Hinckley. An Arab Muslim who keeps a picture of the Pope on the wall of his Beirut office, Khashoggi proved that he could even embrace the conservative Mormons if there were money to be made. More important, though, was the fact that the Mormons were, apparently, returning his embrace.

Khashoggi's philanthropy in Utah, like his business deals, later brought him a new round of negative publicity. Officials at the Latter Day Saints Hospital to which Khashoggi had made a major charitable commitment accused him of providing only $300,000 of a pledge of more than $1 million. Similar charges were made by the Salt Lake City Ballet Company. According to the general manager, Khashoggi, through his firm Triad America, pledged $150,000 in support of the new production "Abdallah," a tale from *The Arabian Nights*. Assuming that the commitment was solid, the ballet company had borrowed the money from a local bank. When only $50,000 arrived, it had to cut back both its budget and its schedule.

The outcry that followed included not only charges of tainted generosity or questions about his motives, but also the accusation that Khashoggi failed consistently to deliver on philanthropic commitments.

At American University, however, President Berendzen reported that Khashoggi had kept to his schedule in making payments on his pledge. The gift was not only in cash, but straightforward and unencumbered. Oil prices were falling and Khashoggi's net worth was diminishing. Whether or not he was still the richest man in the world, it was clear that both his financial empire and the goodwill he once enjoyed were in danger of crumbling.

In spite of his changing fortunes, Khashoggi continued his busy schedule and his romance of the rich and famous. He flew about three-quarters of a million miles a year, and to maintain his arduous schedule, he rarely slept more than four hours a night. He was in perfect health and always full of energy. In addition to his business deals and his lavish entertaining, with beautiful women flown in from around the world, each day also included a daily massage and adjustments to his spinal column by chiropractors. He complained that the label "arms dealer" was unfair, and instead compared himself to the chairman of Lockheed and other companies in the weapons business who were not, he noted, so stigmatized.

In their book, *The Rockefellers*, authors Peter Collier and David Horwitz make the claim that great wealth often comes as an accident.

Writing about John D. Rockefeller, they said, "It was as if a door had stood open for a brief moment and Rockefeller, who just happened to be passing by, managed to squeeze in before it closed." While this may have been too simple an explanation of circumstances and conditions far more complex, it is worth noting that Khashoggi once attributed his wealth to "being in the right place at the right time."

But Rockefeller managed to hold onto his wealth and see it grow to the point that the charitable side continued to cast a large shadow in perpetuity. This may not be the case with Khashoggi. The dramatic fall in OPEC oil exports that began in 1982 has produced a tremendous reduction in revenues for the Kingdom of Saudi Arabia. This in turn has led to a period of painful economic retrenchment. After several years of indecision by King Fahd and of fruitless waiting for oil prices to rebound, the government has moved strongly to bring spending in line with cash flow. One of the first areas to feel the budget axe has been the military, which was treated so lavishly during the period in which Khashoggi acquired his fortune.

This belt-tightening in military expenditures and in the country at large seems to have undercut one of Khashoggi's most significant streams of income, but arms dealing remains a lucrative industry. A study sponsored by the Rockefeller Foundation and other private groups reported that the nations of the world spent nearly $900 billion on weapons in 1986. This was a historic high of $1.7 million per minute, employing about 100 million people, and representing about six percent of the world's gross standard product. This compares to an estimated $800 billion of military spending in 1985 and more than $14 trillion since 1960.

Of the 140 countries listed in the Rockefeller-funded study, Saudi Arabia ranked third, behind only the United States and the Soviet Union, ahead of the United Kingdom, France, the Federal Republic of Germany, and China. And so while the Saudis have been cutting back on military spending, their expenditures are still high enough to continue to generate wealth for the middleman.

Yet the standard of living in Saudi Arabia is clearly on the decline. The present reduction in oil revenues is not simply short-term. Economists project that the need for austerity will last into the early 1990s, when dwindling non-OPEC oil resources will begin to restore to Saudi Arabia and other key Middle East countries much of their lost power to set oil prices and control oil markets.

All of this has led to speculation that Khashoggi has been cut adrift from his most secure lifeline. His extravagant life-style at a time when even the royal family was adjusting its standard of living has most assuredly caused disquietude. Moreover, the publicity over the Iran arms-for-hostages deal and his financial troubles in Utah and elsewhere have all served to taint Khashoggi's image as a dealmaker and financier, as well as philanthropist.

So what are we to make of Khashoggi's generosity? Has he reinterpreted the Bedouin ethic of hospitality and the charitable tradition of Islam to fit the special contours of his highly controversial world? His motives appear to be mixed at best. There is clearly an intent to improve his public image, and while this may not be too different from the motives of others who are even more celebrated for their largesse, it does raise questions about the relationship between the giver and the gift. There is no doubt that both Khashoggi and American University, for example, have benefited from his contribution to the sports complex. In receiving the gift, the university has bestowed upon Khashoggi a measure of respectability. At the same time, in making the gift he has provided the university with the capacity to achieve its academic objectives. Yet, even those who regard Khashoggi's gift as morally neutral are bound to be taken aback by the university president's assertion that Khashoggi "has exemplified at our university the true meaning of the word philanthropy: to love mankind."

The love may or may not be tainted, but it is certainly tempered: American University gets a badly needed sports complex and Khashoggi gets his name immortalized in steel and his largesse nationally acclaimed. But even in these bad times, when he is beleaguered by creditors and the collapse of his biggest deals, Khashoggi continues to believe the lesson on charity he first learned from his father on that hot summer day in his eighth year: compassion should be tempered with logic and logic tempered with compassion. This time, however, he must undoubtedly hope that some of the compassion will be toward him.

12

Ryoichi Sasakawa
Japan

IT WAS 4:30 IN THE MORNING. The streets of Tokyo were still dark, but an 86-year-old industrialist was starting his morning jog. Hours later, Ryoichi Sasakawa offered a penetrating view of the paradoxes that surround his personality and his philanthropy. "While I am jogging, the moon is in the heavens, I say 'thank you.' When I run, I say hello to the flowers. I pray for the birds. I feel thanks to even the leaves on the trees. I pray to God, express gratitude to him." He went on to acknowledge: "I know and feel the presence of omnipotence, but I am not a fanatic to any religion."

This reverence for all forms of life and the willingness to borrow from all forms of religion are but two of the many qualities that set Sasakawa apart from other philanthropists whose benevolence is also legend. A man of considerable contrasts, he has been described as a gambling czar, stock market operator, humanitarian, political power broker, sportsman, suspected war criminal, rightist agitator, and patriot. Estimates of his wealth vary from a "mere" $60 million to billions. Revered by world leaders for his global largesse, he is resented by some Japanese who take exception to his very public philanthropy. They argue that public attention to private acts of benevolence is not a part of Japanese culture. Others dislike the fact that his philanthropy is made possible by gambling.

The controversy surrounding Sasakawa's charitable giving is not limited to Japan. The August 10, 1986 edition of the *Sunday Times* of London described him as a close friend of Sun Myung Moon, head of the Unification Church, whose members are commonly known as "Moonies." A number of British groups strongly objected when Sasakawa was asked to underwrite the deficit incurred by the Edinburgh Commonwealth Games. The chairman of the Games, Robert Maxwell, issued a statement disavowing the Moonies, but welcoming Sasakawa's financial support.

A 1978 U.S. government report, "Investigation of Korean–American Relations," also mentions Sasakawa's links with the Moonies. According to the *Sunday Times,* "In the name of anti-communism, Moon's followers allied themselves with powerful right-wing figures in Japan, such as Ryoichi Sasakawa." In 1985, Moon was jailed for tax offenses in the United States.

What is the truth about Sasakawa? Is there such a thing as tainted generosity? The prewar fascism of the man everyone calls "Mr. Sasakawa" is generally acknowledged, but so are his more recent contributions "to making the world a better place." It is true that he spent three years in jail as a war-crimes suspect, but it is also true that he has been responsible for millions of dollars of contributions to the World Health Organization to support the fight to wipe out leprosy and other dreaded diseases in the developing world. It is true that the money he gives away comes largely from organized gambling on speedboat races, but the professors at Oxford University in England and the black students at Morehouse College in Atlanta, Georgia, have welcomed his benefactions.

Ryoichi Sasakawa was eager to talk about his philanthropy and his past. Obviously, anyone who is responsible for more than $1 billion of philanthropy is no ordinary man; but his willingness to run against the tide of history—demanding that Japan, as a new economic superpower, play a larger role in contributing to the peace and prosperity of the rest of the world—is especially intriguing.

The Japanese heritage is one of strong nationalistic fervor. The Japanese sense of separateness, of being a unique people, does not lend itself easily to internationalism. Moreover, the notion of philanthropy as an expression of an idealized love of humanity has had little place in

Japanese history and culture. Charitable assistance in Japan traditionally has not been directed to the general good of an unknown or anonymous public but for the particular benefit of a private individual, family, or institution with whom the donor shared close personal ties. Japanese historians and theologians even debate whether the Buddhist concept of compassion as "forgetting oneself and benefiting others" is intended to refer to an active virtue like philanthropy.

Generally speaking, formal religion does not have a great deal of personal meaning for Sasakawa, so the journey through the motives and values that shape his largesse must begin elsewhere. Little known in the English-speaking world, the face and profile of Ryoichi Sasakawa are common to all Japanese. Frequently interrupting television programs to peddle his special brand of fitness and charm, he is as much a mystery as he is a man of considerable power—one of Japan's wealthiest tycoons and one of the world's most visible philanthropists. Of the more than $1.35 billion in charitable contributions for which he has been responsible, either directly or indirectly, $214 million has gone to support projects outside Japan. This growing interest in social needs overseas has included support of the (Jimmy) Carter Presidential Center in Atlanta, Georgia, a Ryoichi Sasakawa Fellowship at Harvard University, and the establishment of the U.S.-Japan Foundation, a research-funding organization based in New York.

How did the charitable impulse emerge? What are Sasakawa's motives? How was his commitment to internationalism developed? These were just a few of the questions to which he responded with wit and charm. "When I was eleven years old," Sasakawa offered through an interpreter, "my parents said, 'This is not our child. He was given by the heavens to sweep away the evils of the world.' I have a lot of dirt to sweep." Continuing this imagery, he went on to say, "I was brought up very strictly, very different from my brothers and sisters. While in my heart I complained about the strong discipline, it became very clear to me how I should live."

This notion of having been selected, ordained to a special calling, reflects the sense of mission Sasakawa seems to feel. While he has been accused of being the modern version of the arrogant samurai of the Tokugawa era, he seemed more like a sensitive and delicate descendant of Zen Buddhism.

But why philanthropy? Was there a commitment at an early age? "I have a very sure memory about that point," Sasakawa stated. "I was thirteen years of age—a primary school student. Always on my way to school and back, I saw this lady who appeared to be sewing. She never seemed to move. I wondered why she always stayed home and never went out. At that time, Japanese rural areas regarded an unmarried woman after twenty-three as an old maiden who had lost her chance. This lady appeared to be over thirty but still not married. So I asked my mother why. She said that a cousin in the family was suffering from leprosy, and once you have leprosy in the family women do not have a chance to get married. So I thought, these people are the most suffering and ignored people in the world. Someday I would like to do something."

In May 1974, the Sasakawa Memorial Health Foundation was inaugurated; its primary purpose is the eradication of leprosy. Its founder and benefactor arranged for millions of dollars to be granted to the foundation to relieve the misery of lepers and to combat leprosy throughout the world. Working through the World Health Organization (WHO) and the International Federation of Anti-Leprosy Association (ILEP), Sasakawa, true to his childhood commitment, has been responsible for epochal events in the history of leprosy relief. He is also recognized for bankrolling many of the dramatic achievements that led WHO in 1980 to announce that smallpox had been eradicated and that the scourge of mankind for centuries was no longer a danger to be dreaded.

Born in 1899, the eldest son of a sake (Japanese rice wine) brewer in a remote area of Osaka, Japan, Sasakawa has a remarkable background of industry and intrigue. He made his fortune as a speculator in rice before World War II, and in 1942 he was elected a member of the National Diet of Japan (House of Representatives). After the war, he played an important role in the economic revival of Japan, but the roots of his philanthropy extend back to his days of imprisonment as a suspected war criminal.

While it was difficult to persuade Sasakawa to talk about the war or his three years in a dark prison cell, it was there that he found new meaning and purpose. On January 18, 1946, he wrote a resolution that still guides his life. "The most horrible sin on earth is killing, with war being the paramount example," he said. "Despite the dedicated efforts of numerous people in the cause to end all wars, human history has shown us nothing but a repetition of wars."

"The only way to allow the souls of the war dead to rest in peace is to bring about everlasting peace and rid the earth forever of the horrors of war," he wrote. With this as his philosophy, Sasakawa's philanthropy has come to focus primarily on the principle that the world is one family; all humankind are brothers and sisters. But it is not only the development of his philosophy that distinguishes his years in prison. It was there that he first thought of the process by which the money has been acquired for his benevolence.

What changed Sasakawa from Japanese patriot to world citizen appears to have come about by chance. Although he could not read English, he enjoyed looking at the photographs in the magazines presented by the prison guards in Sugamo prison. One day he was lucky enough to get a copy of *Life* magazine. He was particularly attracted to a photograph of a race of small motorboats. The rest is history, for it has been through his motorboat racing schemes that billions of dollars have been raised to fuel the philanthropy he now enjoys so immensely.

Was this burst of inspiration a charitable impulse or an entrepreneurial instinct? Was he thinking of how best to provide recreative opportunities to uplift the spirit of the Japanese people or was he simply interested in making money? "Neither," was his reply. "After the war Japan had nothing. It is surrounded by the sea. We needed ships in order to survive. So first I thought, how can we rebuild our merchant fleet? We have to reconstruct our ships. So then I thought, what is the shortest cut to restoring our shipbuilding capability? For this we need R&D (research and development), but who is to supply the funds for R&D? Then I thought that public racing might be the best way. But there was already automobile, horseback, and bicycle racing. So the only thing I could think of was motorboat racing. Actually, this has worked out well and supplies a lot of funds for the R&D of our shipbuilding." In the nearly four decades that have elapsed since Sasakawa's imprisonment, his motorboat scheme has worked out quite well indeed—far better than anyone could have imagined. By agreement with the Transport Ministry of Japan, the fans win about 75 percent of the gross total take for motorboat racing; the remainder is split among the sponsoring city, the regional Motorboat Association, and the Japan Shipbuilding Industry Foundation. The foundation was not only Sasakawa's creation, but he serves as chairman of the board. He has also been president of the Motorboat Racing Association since 1955. In these dual capacities, he has acquired an extraordinary amount of economic and political influence.

It is not always clear whether a gift from Sasakawa is from his personal resources or from the Shipbuilding Industry Foundation, but it really does not matter. The foundation has a screening committee, but the final decision on grants is made by Sasakawa and his son, Yohei.

Local Sasakawa critics are concerned about both his power and his publicity. There is much talk of his right-wing (nationalistic) political past, his manipulation of the political process, and the fact that, before the war, he somehow assembled a 15,000-strong black-shirt army—an achievement that remains cloaked in mystery to this day. Yet, it may be his high public visibility as a philanthropist that causes the most concern.

Sasakawa's inclination toward dramatic public action is not new. His unusual action surrounding imprisonment by the American occupation forces as a war criminal is a story told with both humor and incredulity. It seems that he approached the whole affair as something to be celebrated. Dressed in the Japanese attire for the most formal occasion (the "Hakoma" and the "Haori"), he rode up to the prison gate in a car followed by a truck that carried a brass band and a group of drummers. There was also a large banner that read: "A Farewell Celebration for Mr. Sasakawa." To add to the bizarre nature of his imprisonment, it seems to have been a voluntary (or at least premature) act. Designated by the U.S. occupation forces under General Douglas MacArthur as a Class A war criminal, he turned himself in *before* his trial.

But no one should conclude from this story that Sasakawa is an eccentric old man who could easily be dismissed were it not for the more than one billion dollars of philanthropy he has generated. When asked whether there were any extraordinary influences on his life, he told a story about what he learned from his father's experiences as a sake brewer: "It was a small shop on the outskirts of Osaka," he said. "Always, my father dealt with local villagers who came to our house to buy a few bottles of sake. My father used to ask them how many children they have. How were the crops this year? They told him 'good' or 'bad.' My father would then say to them, 'Do not buy two bottles today. You buy only one bottle so you do not waste your income from your work. You cannot keep up your family members that way. Think of your family. Drink one bottle tonight, not two.' They would appreciate the advice and take one bottle with satisfaction."

Sasakawa went on to say that it was this experience that gave him the idea that when you are a seller you should think of the benefit of your purchaser. "Do not always think only of your benefit." He then added with considerable feeling, "This is the way I look at Japan's economy today. As you know, we are experiencing frictions all over the world because, after the war, when Japan started to export our goods, we only tried to make our own benefits—our own living. Our economists never thought of how the purchaser might suffer unemployment and all the worst effects. They thought only of Japan's benefit." Touching on one of the very sensitive points in Japan's emergence as an economic superpower, Sasakawa voiced his own optimism that as an economically successful country that has renounced war, Japan has the opportunity to lead the way in establishing peace and understanding among the peoples of the world.

The search for a deeper cause for Sasakawa's motives and values returned to the subject of religion. Was his compassion, his benevolence, rooted in a moral tradition? "No, I have no religion, no specific religion, but I am not an atheist," he answered. This coincides with the claim of students of Japanese culture that, generally speaking, religion has come to occupy only a peripheral position in Japanese life. A number of religions coexist. They are deeply embedded in the Japanese culture, but most Japanese tell you they have no interest in religion. A public opinion poll conducted by the *Asahi Shimbun* newspaper revealed that 36 percent of the respondents professed some faith, while the remainder did not. By religion, 27 percent identified themselves as Buddhists, 4 percent as followers of Shinto, 2 percent as Christians, 2 percent as adherents of both Buddhism and Shintoism, and 1 percent as followers of some other faith.

The secularism of Japanese society may be an accepted fact, but even a casual observance would suggest that religion is still a highly visible presence in Japanese life. Not only do Shinto shrines and Buddhist temples abound, but the religious rites—Shinto marriages, Buddhist funerals, and even altars in the home—suggest that many Japanese still find meaning in religious symbols and observances.

Sasakawa may not be inclined to a specific religion, as he put it, but like many of his countrymen he has borrowed from and been heavily influenced by native Japanese religious inspiration. After professing that he was not religious, he went on to say, "Yet I believe that what we do on this earth should be rewarded or punished. So when I see people suffering from disease or whatever, I try to help them. I also believe in the presence of omnipotence. I pray regularly. I pray for human beings, but not exclusively—sometimes for the beasts and birds, that they stay away from suffering."

When he talked about his motives for philanthropy, Sasakawa's mysticism gave way to a remarkable pragmatism. "Government taxes assets but it cannot tax achievements. I decided a long time ago that when I die, I will leave only achievements—no assets. That is why none of my family members will inherit even a penny from what I have. That is why I have no personal interest in material things."

In his office, surrounded by pictures of his father with the Pope, the Queen of England, President Jimmy Carter, and other world leaders, Sasakawa's son Yohei also spoke of a creed of austerity and the fact that he would not inherit any money. He remembers two gifts from his father—$2 once and $10. What he inherits, he suggested, is his father's commitment to austerity and his concern for others. Once, for example, when Yohei was hospitalized, his father visited all of the patients, not just his son.

Sasakawa described the astonishment of his friend Jimmy Carter when he saw the simplicity of the Sasakawa home. "When I met Jimmy Carter for the first time several years ago, he said, 'When you come to the United States come to Plains and stay at my home. When I visit Japan I will stay in your home.' When he visited Japan three years ago, he came to my house for lunch, but once he stepped inside, he was surprised. He thought I was living in a huge mansion, considering what I have done in philanthropy. When I heard this, I told him that throughout the world we have so many people who are suffering poverty, and shortages of food. Many people die without receiving the benefit of modern medicine. So why should I live luxuriously and waste my money? I rather spend it for philanthropic causes."

Sasakawa's ideas seem at times to parallel those of the Chinese philosopher Son Tsu, who believed that everything that exists has meaning. The basic idea that the spirit can be found in everything is close to Shintoism. He even shares with the small group of Christians in Japan the idea of charity as a moral duty. Like most of his countrymen, he does not accept the idea so prevalent in the West that a person has to adhere exclusively to one religion or another. He does not follow a religious tradition, but he is a product of Buddhism and Shintoism, Confucianism and Christianity.

Sasakawa is convinced that compassion is not limited by race or nationality, nor by creed. While a man of considerable power, he believes that compassion embodies an ideal of human relations in which all people are on a completely equal footing. In talking to others in Japan about the roots of Sasakawa's benevolence, specifically the influence of religion, there are those who argue that in both Buddhism and Shintoism human existence is regarded as a temporary condition. The focus is on right-living in order to earn merits for the afterlife, but right-living (merit-making) is identified more with personal obedience than with public obligation.

Yet there are followers of Buddha who insist that compassion is a key element of Buddhist teaching. They point to two sanskrit terms: *maitri*, meaning friendship and loving kindness, and *karuna*, meaning sympathy and understanding. Compassion is therefore interpreted as the quality of conferring happiness and saving sentient beings from suffering. The founder of the Tendai sect in Japan (Saicho, 767–822 A.D.), is especially remembered for having defined Buddhist compassion as "forgetting one's self and benefiting others." The October 1985 bulletin of the Niwano Peace Foundation in Japan argues that just as the precept against taking life expresses a passive virtue, so does compassion embody an active Buddhist virtue.

Sasakawa is firmly convinced that while peace must be his primary pursuit, the effort to abolish arms is not enough. Endeavors must be made to achieve a life free from want, illness, and injustice for all humankind in order to bring about permanent peace. He is a great admirer of Martin Luther King, Jr., in this regard. "When I think of the United States, always the name of Martin Luther King strikes my heart," he said. When asked why, he responded, "Because he is the one who really performed what he believed. He did not care for any kind of oppression. He sacrificed himself in order to eradicate injustice in the world. I really admire the American people for making his birthday a national holiday. This is one thing the people of the United States can be proud of in the world. This is a sign that the United States really wants—and is chasing after—peace in the world."

Sasakawa's critics argue that the purpose of his highly visible philanthropy is to secure the Nobel Peace Prize, for which he has been twice nominated. He and his supporters insist that his preoccupation with peace comes out of his belief in the brotherhood and sisterhood of humankind. It also appears that his experience of war and the legacy of isolation have been significant factors. In one year, 1983, he was responsible for more than $25 million in grants for international purposes. A 1985 report on the overseas support and assistance of the Japan Shipbuilding Industry Foundation, which Sasakawa heads, lists $49 million in contributions to the United Nations and $100 million directly to selected countries, including the establishment of foundations in Scandinavia, Britain, and the United States.

Former British Prime Minister Edward Heath said of Sasakawa: "His energy is immense; his personal interest in both Japanese and world affairs is intense; his wish to insure a more orderly and peaceful relationship between countries shines out in all he does; his enjoyment of life, surrounded as he is by a happy family, is clear for all to see—indeed it is as infectious as his sense of humor."

Sasakawa will probably continue to have his detractors as well as his supporters, but for the many people in both the developing and the developed world who have benefited from his largesse, the issue is closed. Ryoichi Sasakawa is one of a kind. Most philanthropists, present and past, have had a national bias. Sasakawa seeks to help the world as a whole, irrespective of geography, ideology, or political or religious consideration. That is the measure of the man. It eclipses questions about his right-wing politics, his usually public philanthropy, the source of the funds he distributes, and his exercise of behind-the-scenes political power.

The Japanese people's sense of unease with Sasakawa may be due to his former ties with Admiral Isoroku Yamamoto, the architect of the Pearl Harbor bombing, or even to the prevailing sense that gambling money is unclean. Yet the money he controls, either directly or indirectly, may help to stamp out many of the dreaded problems of our day, while also finding solutions to the problems a badly divided world will face in the next century. The man who says hello to the flowers has also left his calling card at the doors of those who work for peace and human understanding.

PART FIVE

The Benevolent
Community

13

A Final Look at Motives

A FINAL LOOK AT MOTIVES is now in order. These profiles have been grouped according to themes that fit into four dominant typologies: 1) civic duty, 2) moral imperatives, 3) the search for meaning, and 4) mixed or tainted generosity. The emphasis has been on the most altruistic benefactors. Nevertheless, the impulses that give rise to acts of generosity in other cultures are as varied as those that have been identified in the United States by Warren Weaver in *U.S. Philanthropic Foundations*,[1] Joseph C. Goulden in *The Money Givers*,[2] and the researchers who contributed to the Council on Foundations' study, *America's Wealthy*.[3] The one major exception is the absence of tax incentives abroad; only a very few countries provide tax inducements of any kind. Moreover, many countries use their tax systems to discourage or greatly limit the accumulations of wealth and the excess cash that makes significant contributions possible.

THE OTHER SIDE OF ALTRUISM

Rarely is there a single reason for acts of generosity. Among the additional motives identified in this study, some of the most obvious include the following:

Advancing the social status of the donor

Charitable giving in most cultures is tied to the notion of personal mod-

esty or even anonymity on the part of the giver. Some donors managed
to use their largesse to advance their social status, achieve wide recognition, or advance their family name. Much of the objection to Ryoichi
Sasakawa in Japan can be traced to the attention he has brought to himself and his philanthropy.

Obtaining public attention for charitable acts has sometimes served
to dramatize a need or even encourage others to emulate a benefactor.
But the case of explicit emphasis by the donor on his donation is of a different character. The public relations agents of Adnan Khashoggi made
certain that his philanthropy was clearly associated with the Khashoggi enterprises or that it was used to dispel negative publicity about
Khashoggi himself.

Some donors obviously set out to purchase social prestige or to
achieve a form of personal immortality. William Morris, who became
Lord Nuffield, arrived in Oxford with little public notice and no public
stature whatsoever. He set out to win the respect of university dons and
ended up winning the respect of a grateful society. After outright rejection by the local social elite, he first endowed an academic chair and later
a college. A few years later, he had won every award Oxford University
had to offer. His crowning benefaction, the Nuffield Foundation,
ensured that even future generations would honor and respect his
memory.

The desire to achieve corporate immortality

To ensure that the businesses that brought them wealth survived their
death, some owners created an ownership structure based on what we
have come to know as the private foundation model. Their motive was
to avoid a complete loss of control by the donor, his family, or his associates. The Bernard van Leer Foundation's ownership of the van Leer
enterprises headquartered in Amsterdam added a different twist, however. In this case, a foundation was set up to receive and control a con-
tainer manufacturing business to avoid "the disadvantage of eventual
inexpert...family control."

In the United States, there are now specific legal provisions that limit
the business holdings of a private foundation to a noncontrolling interest. This is not the case in most other countries. The Tata charitable

trusts in India own more than 80 percent of the stock in the parent firm, Tata Sons, of which Tata Industries, the largest industrial group in India, is a 100 percent subsidiary. The Wellcome Trust in England was created by the will of Sir Henry Solomon Wellcome, who at the time of his death was the sole proprietor of the worldwide pharmaceutical business of Burroughs Wellcome and Company. Under the terms of his will, all of the assets of the company were vested in the trustees of the foundation, who were to use the profits for specified charitable purposes. In Denmark, J. C. Jacobsen, who established the Carlsberg Brewery, bequeathed his business to the Carlsberg Foundation.

While some of the legal structures providing for corporate immortality were created after the death of the donor—and cannot, therefore, be attributed to a personal motive for benevolence—others, like Lord Nuffield, specifically sought to secure the stability of their businesses while avoiding any large windfall for the government. In a letter describing Nuffield's motives for creating the Nuffield Foundation, his lawyer defined one of his aims as that of "securing the stability of Morris Motors by eliminating first, market fluctuations caused by any mass movement of the equity and, secondly, changes in management brought about by equity stockholders who have acquired holdings large enough to produce such changes."[4]

Enlightened self-interest

Enlightened self-interest is the idea that a charitable act that benefits the recipient will also redound to the advantage of the donor, either indirectly or in the future. Welfare capitalism, in which owners/employers in widely divergent societies used a portion of their profits to meet the needs or improve the well-being of their workers, was an example of enlightened self-interest. Community philanthropy, in which industrialists set out to make workers more productive by making their communities more satisfying, came to reflect another form of enlightened self-interest. Even philanthropy that sought to contribute to national development or national independence served to ensure the stability needed to accumulate wealth and/or develop new markets.

Few philanthropists spoke as directly about enlightened self-interest as Harry Oppenheimer, who sought to appeal to both the economic self-interest of the South African business community (mostly English) and the political self-interest of the people who dominated public policy (mostly Afrikaner). His appeal to self-interest often worked where appeals to moral values and humanitarianism did not. Similarly, Calouste Gulbenkian's definition of self-interest differed widely from others in the Armenian community, but he had hopes that his benefactions would redound either to his advantage or to that of his community.

There were also many examples of private largesse based on implicit exchange or reciprocity. It was sometimes expected that a gift to the favorite charity of another donor would result in a return gift to one's own charity. Some economists would describe such an exchange as a barter transaction in the framework of self-interest rather than simply an altruistic or charitable act. Reciprocity, however, was the dominant motive for many important benefactions, and it probably demonstrates the necessary distinction between enlightened self-interest and a narrower, more selfish interest.

Promoting ideas or advocating a particular point of view

The contemporaries of Polly van Leer, both in Israel and elsewhere, quickly learned that the influence of money on ideas can be powerful. She doggedly sought to shape the thinking of her time, to persuade intellectuals—men and women of letters and policymakers—that a new metaphysics was not only possible but highly desirable. Joseph Rowntree and George Cadbury combined firmly held ideas with financial support for a new understanding of the responsibilities of wealth and the role of private philanthropy.

Lord Nuffield was not only a systematic, strategic philanthropist but his efforts to promote an idea often went beyond merely conferring a grant; accompanying his gifts were well-reasoned prescriptions as to their use. A successful entrepreneur, he sought in his philanthropy to promote the principles and practices of private enterprise.

It should not be assumed, however, that most philanthropists who sought to promote ideas did so because of any ingenuous or arrogant confidence in their own ideas. In most cases, it was their confidence in the ideas of others that persuaded them that new knowledge in certain fields would be particularly helpful to their communities. Eugenio Mendoza's support of research into the most dreaded diseases in Venezuela was the result of such a view.

A means of paying conscience money or restoring respect to a maligned family name

Fritz Thyssen funded Adolf Hitler early in his rise to power. Although he later disavowed national socialism and the Third Reich, he was on the bandwagon at a critical moment. Upon his death, his widow created the Thyssen Foundation. She was assisted in this effort by officials of the Ford Foundation, who were seeking ways to enable war-torn Germany to rebuild both its cultural life and its national life. In creating the foundation, the Thyssen family sought to restore and relate the family name to more favorable causes.

Continuing a family tradition

Some philanthropists were members of a "leading family" that had been known for its beneficence and public spiritedness for generations. This was especially true of families whose wealth and attitude toward philanthropy were inherited. Many members of the second and third generations are intentionally following in the footsteps of their parents and grandparents. Others, like Harry Oppenheimer, could not have avoided the family comparison and public expectation under any circumstance. His father, Ernest Oppenheimer, is remembered for taking on the problems of separate development more than fifty years before the formal policy of apartheid was developed and implemented.

COMMON FEATURES

A final look at the public spirit of the benefactors described throughout this book suggests that, while their methods and motives were varied, there are common features that stand out.

Community

The most prominent common characteristic was the experience of being a part of a community. The beneficence of most of the donors expanded as their sense of community expanded, often evolving from a very narrow view to embrace a larger universe. In many societies, the notion of community was limited to a close-knit family structure. The sense of mutual obligation within the family, clan, or social group did not normally extend to those outside the group. Despite the emphasis of some of our donors on obligations to an enlarged human family, there remained, for many of their contemporaries, an indifference to the needs and wants of those outside their primary community. Yet the growth of philanthropy may be measured by the extent to which the notion of community obligations came to include outsiders (the poor, slaves, even enemies) whose fate was previously a matter of little or no concern.

What was unique about those in these pages who forged a new philanthropic order was their ability to make the leap from individual growth and small-group community to an expanding notion of community. And as the experience of community expanded, so did the practice of philanthropy. Jamsetji Tata's concern for his fellow Parsis grew to include his employees, their communities, and ultimately all of India. Many benevolent industrialists started out with a form of welfare capitalism—using their profits to improve the quality of life of their employees—and ended up seeking to strengthen or sustain larger communities. Members of a ruling class elite, many philanthropists came eventually to use their wealth to empower people outside the mainstream of their communities. There was a sense that for every person rescued from the margins of society, a direct value was added to the lives of those in the mainstream.

Practicality

It is also worth noting that, for most of the donors, philanthropy was practical; it was a calculated attempt to use wealth to achieve one or more specific charitable objectives. Angela Burdett-Coutts was eulogized as a benevolent woman who believed in judicious charity. Joseph Rowntree believed that benevolence was likely to be more effective if it was the product of rational analysis as well as emotional feeling. Lord Nuffield came to be described by those who knew him as a practical, methodical man in both business and philanthropy.

Eugenio Mendoza and Jamsetji Tata also believed in practical philanthropy. Mendoza responded personally and immediately to those needs that moved him, but he used foundations and other forms of institutional philanthropy to analyze, contemplate, and support long-term solutions. It was Tata's belief that philanthropy should be practical and constructive that led him to go beyond the traditional alms-giving of his fellow Parsis to set up a nonsectarian fund for the talented without regard to sect or class.

It can thus be said of most of this diverse group that, while distant from each other in geography and time, they nevertheless shared the distinction formally made between charity and philanthropy. Charity was largely affective and more likely to be ad hoc and episodic, while philanthropy was more cognitive, generally more calculated and systematic.

Professionalism

The philanthropy of our donors was very personal, but at the same time professional. Angela Burdett-Coutts made philanthropy her profession. She turned to Charles Dickens as her first charitable administrator, but she answered hundreds of letters personally, seeking to fuse good professional advice with her own instincts and personal involvement. The success in enterprise led other philanthropists to apply what they learned in business to their approach to philanthropy. As they sought the best advice available in making production, marketing, and other business decisions, many sought to organize and administer their philanthropy similarly.

The efficient handling of requests for philanthropic assistance was of considerable advantage. Some donors sought to shield themselves from the pressure and nuisance of emotional appeals—using staff as an impersonal screen—but they did not allow that shield to limit their vision or stifle their view of social needs. Some donors clearly preferred to have no formal or legal intermediaries between themselves and the many seekers of their support, yet they still sought to use objective analysis and efficient organization to ensure the maximum impact of their philanthropic dollars. They believed that the best mechanism for giving away money was one that required knowledge, wisdom, and integrity. While most donors would probably have agreed with the concept that philanthropy is more art than science, they also generally believed that the charitable impulse could be enhanced by exposure to acquired skills.

To describe the methods of those we have studied as professional is to describe a willingness to use staff or the advice and counsel of others, learning from the experience of colleagues and those who preceded them, and seeing their philanthropy as both a craft and as what the American industrialist and philanthropist J. Irwin Miller has described as a "calling." As a craft, it had to do with learned skills that enhance the capacity for compassion. As a calling, it had to do with judgment and wisdom. "Calling" begins in selflessness and proceeds through humility and the eagerness to learn, finally bringing the grantmaker to wisdom more directly than by any other path.[5]

The word *professionalism* in this context must not be confused with *credentialism*, the delegation of responsibility to those who assume a knowledge monopoly based on training or credentials. Actually, the word that best describes this early variant of philanthropy is probably *entrepreneurialism;* the emphasis was on flexibility and risk-taking, on judgment and wisdom. This differs greatly from the present tensions between the entrepreneurial and professional subcultures in the Western world, where in philanthropy as in business we romanticize daring and the lack of rigidity, but reward order, security, and that ever-present euphemism, a track record.

Politics

Finally, the practice of philanthropy was often prepolitical. Not only did the sense of public duty precede any incentive or compulsion by government, but active immersion in public life through philanthropy often led to a more direct involvement in the politics of the community. In private life, the donors may have been satisfied with what they could achieve through the uses of their wealth, but once involved in public life, the very experience of trying to help others persuaded some of them of the need for political solutions, strategies, or participation.

Eugenio Mendoza became co-president of Venezeula for a very brief period. He may have been disillusioned by the experience—frustrated by the limitations and inflexibility of the office—but his commitment to the well-being of his country took him eventually into the political sphere. Joseph Rowntree not only set up philanthropic structures to serve charitable purposes, he also bought two London newspapers and actively immersed himself in the political debates of his time. Jamsetji Tata was known for his business acumen and generous spirit, but he also supported the highly political Indian National Congress and was one of the founding members of the Bombay Presidency Association, the leading political association of his time. Lord Nuffield was a very private man, but in his later years he sought to use his influence to shape government policy on economic development, continuing his concern about the underdeveloped regions of Britain. Harry Oppenheimer spent ten years as a member of the South African Parliament. He tried not to mix philanthropy and politics, but his social vision led him to seek political solutions to the problems created by the policy of separate development.

What is remarkable about these philanthropists is how similar their motives and methods were to those of their better-known counterparts in the United States. It has been unfortunate for modern philanthropy that discussions about it are commonly limited to U.S. traditions and practices. There is every reason to expect the continued preeminence of the vehicles of organized philanthropy pioneered by societies and cultures that gave birth to large concentrations of wealth, but it is important to understand and appreciate how philanthropy has thrived in other societies as well.

Inevitably, people must identify role models from the many cultures that will shape the future if human beings are to cultivate compassionate values, promote private giving, and maintain a benevolent community. The men and women described in these pages are representative of countless others whose benefactions are legend in their own communities. Their ranks would certainly include J. C. Jacobsen, who founded the Carlsberg Brewery and established the Carlsberg Foundation in Denmark in 1876, years before the formation of the Ford and Rockefeller foundations in the United States; Adriano Olivetti, a pioneer in corporate social responsibility in Italy; Jaime Carvajal in Colombia, who is described as the personification of the collaboration between the business sector and the nonprofit sector for the good of Latin America; and Fritz Thyssen in Germany, who supported Hitler and the national socialists, but who later wrote: "It is not enough to regret the past—one must profit from the lessons one has learned." The Thyssen Stiftung is now one of the most important and largest philanthropic legacies in Germany.

There are still others, like Andres Barbero in Paraguay, a wealthy physician whose motto was, "It is better to give of oneself than to think of oneself"; Marta Abreu, a woman of extraordinary means whose benefactions were considerable in Nineteenth Century Cuba; Amalita Fortabut, an Argentinian, who is highly regarded locally both for her philanthropy and the fact that she loaned the military her helicopters and planes during the Falkland War; and Henry Dunant, a wealthy Swiss banker who was the founder of the International Red Cross, but whose efforts in behalf of the abolitionists, a Palestinian state for the Jews, and myriad other causes led to bankruptcy.

These men and women, like others in their cultures and communities, felt a sense of interconnectedness between self and society. They acknowledged a debt to those with whom they shared a common space, common needs, and common aspirations. They shared a commitment to a common good that transcended their primary centers of social meaning and belonging and embraced a larger community. We ignore the lessons to be learned from their life stories and the implications for the future of philanthropy at our own peril.

14

Cultivating Compassionate Values

COMPASSION AND GENEROSITY are virtues every society desires to cultivate, but there are all too few clues about how best to prepare the members of the next generation to understand their obligations and meet their responsibilities to one another. The time has come to ask whether it is possible to extrapolate from this study, both the profiles in these pages and the portraits of those researched but not included, certain attributes, values, and even human development practices that can enhance the capacity for compassion or continue the commitment to a benevolent community.

Not all of our donors were motivated by compassionate values, but for those who were there appear to have been at least four stages of consciousness in the evolution of the charitable impulse; stage I, in which compassionate values were developed; stage II, in which compassionate values were nurtured; stage III, in which compassionate values were activated; and stage IV, in which options beyond private benevolence were considered.

The first stage began in the minds of individuals. The values that led to a sense of community or public duty had first to be internalized. In the second stage this transformation of consciousness was externalized. Aristotle once noted that, "Man when perfected is the best of animals, but when separated from law and justice, he is the worst of all." This notion of the humanizing influence of the civil order has its parallel in the idea of intermediary institutions and religious and cultural traditions that reinforce personal values and moral impulses.

The third stage in the evolution of the charitable impulse was the development of a consciousness of a special relationship to other people occupying a common space and sharing a common destiny. This sense of community was often a precondition to the practice of philanthropy. There was a shift from passive to active altruism. The *spirit* of benevolence led to *acts* of benevolence.

A fourth stage of consciousness emerged out of the experience of public life. There developed an awareness of both the limitations of private benevolence and the potential of other forms of public participation or political strategies in achieving the ends desired. For most of our donors, the philanthropic impulse grew to include all four stages of consciousness, while for a few it never did embrace the varieties of public participation implicit in stage IV.

Stage I: The development of an altruistic personality

I was struck in this investigation by the degree to which private beneficence was a part of a family culture. Compassionate values were taught by the family during early childhood. As children, some of the donors were admonished by an elder to treat others well, to be concerned about the well-being of those with whom they shared a special relationship, and to give as much as they got from society. They seemed to have passed through the three "foundation stones" of moral leadership described by Michael Schulman and Eva Mekler in *Bringing Up a Moral Child:* the internalization of parental standards, the development of empathy, and the formation of personal standards.[6]

On the one hand, families that gave primacy to self-interest in the uses of their wealth inculcated in their children such values as personal freedom and personal gratification. On the other hand, those who were more preoccupied with group interests (religion, race, nationality, for example) tended to stress and cultivate cooperation, continuity, and commitment. A third group sought to transmit the values of piety, reverence, and compassion. It was this latter group that were more likely to regard religion as the primary source of values, with some making no distinction between philanthropy and "religion-in-action." Somewhere in the process of their development, the notion of a civic obligation became so rooted in their innermost sense of identity that philanthropy became not simply a moral imperative, but a natural, almost automatic act.

While the best time for teaching compassion and generosity is in childhood, Ervin Staub and others warn that simply espousing altruistic values within the family is not sufficient. There is a specific pattern of childrearing that seems to encourage beneficence in later years. Parents who transmit altruism most effectively exert a firm control over their children's moral development. They actively guide them to do good, to share, to be helpful. Children who have been coached to be helpful are more likely to be helpful when a spontaneous situation arises later.[7] No intermediary institution, regardless of how influential or persuasive, can ever replicate the parent-to-child transmission of compassionate values.

So the first message of these profiles is that the ability to maintain a caring society does not so much lie in the philanthropic institutions we create or even the legacies we bequeath, but in our progeny. Our children must learn from us at an early age that if the strong exploit the weak, or the rich ignore the needy, the future of our society is gravely impaired.

Stage II: The reinforcement of compassionate values

Compassionate values taught by the family in early childhood were often reinforced later by religion, intermediary institutions, or what Robert Reich calls "morality tales" and "cultural parables."[8] These tales and parables, which can be found in every culture, constitute a set of orienting ideas less rigid than an ideology but also less ephemeral than the "public mood."[9] They may be rooted in religion, literature, or indigenous mythology, but they help to shape a common set of moral assumptions. The Poor Laws of England and the notion of charity that emerged in the Seventeenth Century are good examples of how commonly held views about poverty shaped the benevolence of the period. The evangelical zeal of the Protestant Reformation dominated the moral landscape, greatly influencing how an English nobleman viewed the prime question of the time: Is the misfortune of the pauper his own due, and thus a personal tragedy to be mitigated, or is it a social problem to be resolved and a condition to be eliminated? In many Christian camps, poverty was presumed to be a permanent condition. Thus, when private beneficence sought to eradicate poverty through human endeavor, it was going against a widely held view and long tradition; but it was this conception of social progress that helped to introduce the modern notion of philanthropy.

Many of the men and women profiled in these pages were influenced by religious teachings and morality tales that helped them to make sense of and bring coherence to their desire to be helpful. In addition, their own life stories have in many places become the vehicles of public myth and cultural parables. The legends and legacies of Calouste Gulbenkian, for example, are retold in many different versions. The same is true of Polly van Leer and countless men and women not in these profiles whose benevolence speaks to the essence of the self-image of others.

The injunctions of religion are particularly valuable in reinforcing compassionate values because they embody mythologies that are not powered by culture alone. The individual in the very act of accepting the claims of a religious faith transcends the limits of time and culture. Thus, he or she is free to accept and affirm a moral obligation or purpose that may be quite different from what is commonly acted or practiced in his or her own time.

The reinforcement of compassionate values by religion was especially important in cultures where adherents to some religious beliefs found themselves at odds with the prevailing values and assumptions; the Parsi in India and the Quaker in England, for example. The moral imperatives instilled in childhood were likely to have more staying power where they were echoed by religion. But while the commitment to the community is constant in religion, the form that commitment takes varies. It may be a community in microcosm, withdrawn or set apart from a larger society, or it may see itself as coterminous with the body politic, called to serve and transform it at the same time. It is thus instructive to look at how one religious group has responded to cultural situations that either reaffirmed or rejected the moral theology they proclaimed and sought to practice.

Richard Niebuhr's exposition of the relationship between Christianity and society has implications for the Jew, the Muslim, and others acting out of the values and assumptions of their faith as well. Niebuhr in his classic book, *Christ and Culture,*[10] suggested that one could discern in both history and contemporary life five distinct forms of relationships:

1. *Christ against culture,* the posture of withdrawal and retreat as represented in monastic orders and various sects. The withdrawal is either physical, by outright isolation, or spiritual.

2. *Christ of culture,* the idea that there is fundamental agreement between the Church and society. Religion should be providing comfort rather than creating conflict, reinforcing the public life rather than challenging it.

3. *Christ above culture,* suggesting that there are transcendent values that human aspirations can approximate but not fully attain.

4. *Christ and culture in paradox,* an approach that acknowledges the validity of the claim of both religion and society on the individual and the community, while also recognizing the inevitable tensions that come from fundamental contradictions.

5. *Christ transforming culture,* the view of Augustine, Calvin, and others who believed that human nature is perverted and must be redeemed and restored to its essential goodness. Social activism of all sorts has emanated from this view of the relationship of religion and society.

The "religion transforming society" view was a major element in the motivation of those who gave birth to modern philanthropy. They rejected the belief of some of their contemporaries that poverty was a permanent condition unchangeable by human intervention. Moreover, they refused to be private people. Their compassion and concern were developed and reinforced through the public myths or private teachings of their religion.

While religion has been the most powerful force creating and sustaining compassionate values, it would be a mistake to assume that it has been the only one. Mendoza was not a religious man, yet his life and philanthropy reflected all of the noble virtues taught by religion, except piety. Nuffield did not have any religious motives or affiliation whatsoever, but because of his public benefactions he is revered as highly as many of the great men of religion in English history. Both Mendoza and Nuffield had a dynamic and driving sense of the public and their responsibility to it, but they did not care much for the deeper questions of meaning, the saving of souls, creating a new moral order or any of the other elements of the language of moral theology. Both were nationalists who felt a responsibility to contribute something as meaningful, significant, and even as extraordinary in their time as those in the generations that preceded them.

Stage III: The movement from empathy to engagement

Each culture has its triumphant individuals who either live out the ideals of their society more perfectly or rebel against prevailing mythology more completely. The American myth is the story of the little guy who works hard, takes risks, believes in himself, and eventually earns wealth, fame, and honor.[11] This notion of individualism, which was so romanticized in Nineteenth Century America, never reached the same level of deification in other societies. In many other cultures, the person is not, technically speaking, so much an individual as he is a social animal dependent on and responsible to the group. The Japanese, for example, are much more likely than Westerners to operate in groups, or at least to see themselves as operating this way. Where Westerners may at least put on a show of independence and individuality, most Japanese will be quite content to conform in dress, conduct, style of life, and even thought, to the norms of their group.[12] There are signs of change in modern Japan, even convergence with the West, but the attitude toward both the group and private philanthropy will continue for some time to reflect the older, deep-rooted, unconscious belief that it is the group—as now represented by the government or the business corporation—rather than the individual that has responsibility for the common good.

The idea of community benevolence—of those in the mainstream looking out for those on the margins—imposes not only a private sentiment but also a social responsibility on all members of the community. But how is this responsibility to be communicated and maintained?

Eugenio Mendoza was a Venezuelan patriot, first and foremost, but his passion was not simply for defending freedom's privileges, but for extending freedom's benefits. His commitment to a public life with civic responsibilities was the product of a family commitment that went back to the original progenitor, Simón Bolívar, the South American liberator. But his idea of a public life in philanthropy concomitant with a private life in business was not narrowly identified with government officials, civil servants, politics, or government institutions. For him, the notion of a public responsibility was fundamental to his vision of himself and his community. To recognize that he was a member of the public was to recognize that he was not just a member of a special family with special obligations, but that there was an essential oneness, an interdependence between him and those with whom he shared the resources and destiny of his national community.

But how do future Mendozas or any members of a future generation come into such an intense awareness of their interconnectedness that they feel compelled to use their resources to bring a shared vision into being? Most people only experience the unity of the public in moments of high drama:

> Sometimes we recognize the public in a crisis: a President is murdered, November 22, 1963; or the threat of war, Pearl Harbor Day. Sometimes an emergency jars us out of comforting routines: a forest fire, a riot. Or the public becomes visible on those rare occasions when we are challenged by a common heritage and destiny: that August afternoon before the Lincoln Memorial and Martin Luther King, Jr., saying, "I have a dream."

In those moments that which divides us falls away and, for once, seems pitifully unimportant. And then we know, if only in part, that in some inexplicable way we do belong to one another, the mighty and the weak, the rich and the poor alike.[13]

This statement by leaders of the United Presbyterian Church, U.S.A. reflects what M. Scott Peck describes as creating community by crisis. The problem is that once the crisis is over, so—virtually always— is the community. The collective spirit goes out of the people as they return to their ordinary individual lives, and community is lost.[14] Since the experience of true community is almost a prerequisite to philanthropy, creating community by deliberate design must be of concern to those who seek to maintain or cultivate a caring society. And here Peck again has much to say that is helpful. His basic conclusions are these:

1. The words "communicate" and "community," although verb and noun, come from the same root. The principles of good communications are the basic principles of community-building. And because people do not naturally know how to communicate, because humans have not yet learned how to talk with each other, they remain ignorant of the laws or rules of genuine community.
2. In certain situations people may unconsciously stumble onto the rules of communication or community. Since the process is unconscious, however, people do not consciously learn these rules as a result and therefore immediately forget how to practice them.
3. The vast majority of people are capable of learning the rules of communication and community-building and are willing to follow them. In other words, if they know what they are doing, virtually any group of people can form themselves into a genuine community.[15]

Peck's central thesis is that the keystone to benevolence is community, but there can be no community without involvement; there can be no involvement without vulnerability; there can be no vulnerability without risk. Thus, building community means taking risks—risks governments sometimes cannot take or the public might not want to take. In the end, it may be the willingness to take risks that distinguishes private philanthropy from public benevolence.

But dollars—the giving away of cash—make poor social cement. They can only create the conditions that may bring a community together; they do not themselves constitute an effective bond. A relationship may be instituted by cash, but an enduring connection is likely to be made in coming together around a need that is truly a community need. It may be the need of some group within the community—rather than the whole community—but a sense of community develops when the association and the transaction bring together significant portions of the community in a way that creates community-wide ownership of that need. When what was "their problem" becomes "our problem" then the transition transforms a mere association into a community.

Stage IV: The awareness of the interdependence of private, public, and political life

Finally, each society has to decide how it will deal with the limits of private benevolence. Those donors who reached the level of consciousness in stage IV came to recognize the interdependence of private, public, and political life. Their awareness of the limit of private largesse led them to search for alternative public strategies and solutions. They came to recognize that a good society depends on the goodness of individuals, but not exclusively or primarily. There must also be sound government, just laws, and institutions that are benevolent and humane. So while the concern for maintaining a caring society must certainly start with altruistic individuals, it cannot stop there. The history of the United States is instructive in this regard. For years, Americans overemphasized the social role of government while underemphasizing the contributions of private institutions and individuals. Now the opposite is true. We unduly exaggerate the contributions and the potential of private voluntarism while understating the legitimate social role of government. The truth is that the uniqueness of American democracy has been the remarkable pragmatism that has seen generation after generation blend tax-supported services with private voluntarism.

Despite dissimilarities in the rhythm of their history, culture, and social vision, the wealthy who chose to be benevolent shared some views of community that were in many ways similar—although often at odds with their own political or economic culture. One such view is the notion of the social contract between a society and its people. Some of the people we met in our cross-cultural probe lacked confidence in the beneficence of either governments or markets, and they seemed to be equally disillusioned with the social role of both. They differed, therefore, from present-day conservatives in Europe and the United States, who argue that the best way to establish justice, expand opportunities, ensure peace, and even to accumulate wealth is to liberate the forces of commerce in a free market. They also differed from the much-maligned stereotypical liberal, who is regularly denounced for supposedly believing in the power of government to correct all of the ills of society. Benevolent wealth most often reflected the pragmatism involved in the notion of three sectors—business; government; and voluntary, nonprofit, charitable institutions—working sometimes independently and at other times in partnership to achieve a common good. The degree of cooperation or independence among these sectors was usually determined by cultural traditions or political ideology, but those who engaged in private acts of beneficence believed that the private side of society had social responsibilities that paralleled those of the public side.

We tend to think of the sectoral division of society as peculiar to the United States, but in almost every country of Western Europe and many countries of the developing world, the concept has a long history. Marion Fremont-Smith's study of foundations and governments makes the point that nonprofit institutions far antedate the emergence of the other two sectors of democratic government and commercial enterprise.[16] The French historian Alexis de Tocqueville greatly romanticized the American society for its voluntary organizations. Historians have often overlooked individuals of goodwill in other societies who have allocated private resources for the public good without either the compulsion of law or the incentive of profit.

In its earliest application, the notion of sectors referred to a business sector driven by profits, a government sector driven by the ballot, and a third sector driven by compassion. But when private giving moved beyond charity to the protection of the environment and other activities that could not readily make the love of humankind a central objective, the idea of a third sector driven by compassion began to lose its currency. As Daniel Bell argues in *The Coming of Post-Industrial Society,* "What is public and what is private and what is profit and what is not-for-profit is no longer an easy distinction."

There is, admittedly, considerable ambiguity in the idea of three sectors. And it should come as no surprise that these ambiguities are more pronounced in democratic societies. An absolutely totalitarian society would in theory have nothing but an all-embracing government sector, with government equated with the governing power.[17] Thus, large-scale philanthropy of the sort undertaken by the subjects of these profiles is a product of capitalist societies where both large accumulations of wealth and large inequalities are possible.

While wealth made philanthropy possible, it was poverty that first made it necessary. The use of the word *philanthropy* had its genesis in early Greek society, but it was in England during the periods of great contrast between prosperity and poverty that philanthropy really became a part of the lexicon of civic virtues. Sir Francis Bacon wrote in 1595, "Goodness, what the Grecians called philanthropia, is called the greatest virtue." But while it was on European soil that philanthropy first flourished, it was also in England and other European societies that men and women of wealth first came to articulate the limits of private generosity in promoting the general welfare.

With the advent of an urban industrial society and the population explosion that so decisively shaped Nineteenth Century policy, the old social structure and its practices of private benevolence began to show signs of strain and even crisis. Private acts of charity by the benevolent gentlemen and the Victorian ladies who—contrary to popular opinion—frequently escaped from domestic enclaves to run important societies and provide important services, no longer satisfied the aspirations or relieved the tensions of those outside the mainstream economy.

Some years later, the Nathan Commission, established by the British government, went so far as to describe earlier attempts to create by private effort a series of unilateral private responses to social need as "one of the magnificent failures of English history."[18] David Owen, the great historian of English philanthropy, did not go that far, but after observing in his extraordinary study that contributions to the welfare of the state were indispensable, and that motives were both noble and complex, he sought to put the emerging debate on the social role of government in perspective. He argued that as the view of what constitutes a tolerable minimum became less restricted, it became obvious that the major social tasks lay well beyond the resources of private charity, however ambitious and devoted its benefactors. He went on to state the case:

> When the problem was seen as one that, in essentials, had little to do with the actions of individuals, their adequacies and their failures, then the shortcomings of private charity lay exposed. To help individuals handle the unavoidable and grinding poverty of their lives with what success they could, even to assist them in meeting their special crises, was one thing; to ask why and whether the destitution and the evils associated with it were necessary in modern society raised a different order of issue.[19]

One response to the unique problems of the industrial era was the development of the welfare state. Another response was the emergence of a different philosophy of private giving, represented first by Angela Burdett-Coutts in the latter half of the Victorian era and later by industrialists like Joseph Rowntree and George Cadbury. This was the notion that philanthropy would be used to identify and eliminate the cause of social problems rather than simply ameliorate their consequences—the idea that private giving could be used to create a national consciousness of the pervasiveness of a social problem.

The emergence of the antislavery movement in the United States was but one of the many forces that transformed the way in which benevolent wealth was used to address social problems. In England, people like Joseph Rowntree and George Cadbury, who later formed their own private charitable trusts, were among the first to take private philanthropy in two new directions: 1) the voluntary organization of public opinion, and 2) the invention of new means of social advocacy. They sought first to inform and persuade people by the facts of a given subject, and then by the weight of an enlightened public opinion to bring pressure to bear on policymakers.

Thus, the transformation of consciousness that led first to an awareness of the limits of private benevolence also led some benefactors to a fuller immersion in public life. For some, it was the practice of a new form of philanthropy, while others got directly involved in the politics of their time.

15

The Potential and Limits of Private Generosity

PHILANTHROPISTS whose compassionate values took them to the fourth stage of consciousness described in the last chapter went beyond private benevolence and got involved politically because they saw inherent limitations of benevolent wealth in responding to the social needs of their community. They were strong proponents of voluntary action, the social value of individual conscience, and the importance of private initiative to democratic pluralism. But they sought a collective civic commitment capable of generating a consistent stream of resources and setting priorities on the basis of an objective assessment of social needs. They were also concerned about the need for a more systematic and, in some cases, a more equitable commitment to competing needs.

This concern continues among those who seek a benevolent community. The studies of voluntary action in the United States by Lester Salamon led him to argue that philanthropy is limited in its ability to generate an adequate level of resources, is vulnerable to particularism and favoritism, and at times has been associated with amateurism.[20] On the surface, this seems like an unduly negative indictment, but Salamon is in fact pointing to the limitation of voluntary action in order to put it in perspective rather than simply to denigrate it. Using Salamon's reasoning, there are at least four classes of limitations on private largesse as a means of meeting social needs:

Financial insufficiency

The main shortcoming of private benevolence is its inability to generate resources on a scale that is both large enough and consistent enough to cope with the social problems and social needs of an advanced industrial society. Whenever a large share of the burden of coping with the social needs of a society is dependent on private action, it is almost certain that the resources made available will be less than what a truly benevolent community considers optimal. Despite the many excellent contributions by private philanthropy in the United States, for example, the $93 billion given away by Americans in 1987 is pale in comparison with a trillion-dollar federal budget and more than $500 billion in expenditures by state and local governments. Private philanthropy has served the society so well because it has often been carefully targeted for maximum impact, invested the same way we invest our business dollars—to ensure maximum return. Some of the most thoughtful observers of philanthropic practices see effective philanthropy as analogous to the research and development budget of a business corporation. They point out that when the business enterprise uses its research and development money for operating capital, it loses its competitive edge because it no longer has the money needed to develop new products or to refine an existing product line. Thus when private philanthropy becomes maintenance money bailing out endangered institutions, it is no longer available to foster creativity and innovation, to find the cure for dread disease or to objectively consider new public policy options. It is likely to be insufficient as maintenance money, but it can be unusually effective as creative money.

Donor preference

The freedom of the private benefactor to determine which public need is to be met by private largesse is one of the strengths of a democratic society that seeks to inculcate and encourage the charitable impulse. However, it is also true that this particularism has its own weakness. Those who use private resources for public purposes will rarely use their resources to benefit all segments of the community equally. Thus, serious gaps may occur in the coverage of categories of need, as well as groups in need. Particularism can also lead to inefficiencies, contributing to wasteful duplication of philanthropic efforts in some areas and great deficiencies in others.

Donee dependency

Excessive or unusual dependence on private benevolence may vest the influence over defining social needs in the hands of those in command of the greatest resources. The nature of the community's benevolence thus comes to be shaped not by the community but by the wealthy members of the community. The net result may be that those needs favored by the wealthy receive priority attention while those needs most pressing for other members of the community may be overlooked. And even when the needs of the latter group are met, the process by which they are met may create a self-defeating sense that their destiny is really in the hands of those on the giving end.

Sectoral interdependence

The so-called independent sector, so widely celebrated in the United States and the United Kingdom, is not really independent. It has come as a surprise to many Americans to find that government is, and has been for some time, the single most important source of the voluntary sector's income. The 1984 studies by Lester Salamon, then at the Urban Institute, a highly respected U.S. research organization, found that nonprofit organizations received 40 percent of their income from government. By contrast, only 20 percent comes from all types of private giving: individuals, corporations, and foundations.

Government in modern Britain has also increased its payments to charities in the last decade. Like government in the United States, it is now the largest single contributor to the voluntary sector. In 1976, British government sources contributed £175 million of the year's £3,000 million or so in charitable revenue through grants and fees. In 1984, philanthropic revenues had risen to an estimated £10,000 million; government funding had risen to about £1,000 million or 10 percent of this figure. In the 1986 budget, the state further subsidized charitable institutions registered by the Charity Commissioners with a range of fiscal benefits very similar to American-style tax exemptions.[21]

It is an illusion, an extremely dangerous illusion, for any citizens of a democratic society to believe that they can meet the needs of their society by substituting a dependent voluntary sector for an independent government.

Does this suggest, then, that benevolent wealth is of dubious value in maintaining a caring society? Quite the contrary. It emphasizes the importance of developing compassionate values and encouraging private largesse, but it puts philanthropy in perspective by emphasizing that in a truly benevolent community the consensus welfare needs are met by people in common while private benefactors are free to choose which public purpose they will serve. They may choose to provide housing for the homeless. They may choose to feed those who are hungry. They may choose to help heal the sick. But when the intention is to promote the "general" welfare, the well-being of the community cannot be left to the private choices and preference of those who voluntarily choose to be benevolent.

It can thus be argued that there are at least four challenges to those who seek to establish benevolent communities. The first has to do with the tradition of benevolence—how do we maintain the legacy? The second has to do with the practice of benevolence— how do we manage the process? The third has to do with the economics of benevolence—how do we mobilize the resources? And the fourth has to do with the psychology of benevolence—how do we motivate the uncaring and the uncommitted?

The first challenge is primarily conceptual. It grows out of the policy debates in the United States, England, and other nations that have been preoccupied in the 1980s with the social role of government. The decade-long discourse has really been about the nature of the social contract between a society and its people—how shall we solve social problems? How shall we meet social needs? In other words, how shall we build and sustain benevolent communities?

The conceptual problem is one of theory—are private benevolence and the so-called voluntary sector derivatives of the limitations of government, or is government a derivative of the limitations of voluntary action? While this may seem at first to be an abstract argument with limited relevance to AIDS research, hunger in Africa, or ecology in Asia, it is critical to how one views the social role of government and the place of private benevolence in meeting social needs. In the United States, the idea of a third sector of voluntary groups and private philanthropic institutions is gaining credibility. Scholars are busy analyzing it, and colleges and universities are including it among their courses of study. Policymakers are giving it greater scrutiny as a potential source of new revenues, and organizations are springing up to encourage and foster greater collaboration among voluntary groups.

There are dissident voices, however, arguing that the idea of a third sector of private benevolence and voluntary action is a conceptual myth. They point out that communities rose before governments and that private benevolence was regarded as a civic duty or moral imperative before there were political institutions seeking to promote the general welfare. Thus, it is more accurate to describe the diverse array of voluntary action as the first sector rather than the third. Those who see voluntary action as a third sector made necessary by market or government failure are more likely to view private initiatives as a way of filling the gaps created by a limited government. On the other hand, those who see government as a derivative of the limitations of private benevolence are led to seek a larger social role for government.

What is needed is a pragmatic balance, a realism that goes beyond either political ideology or public credo. Maintaining a caring society in those economic and political systems that depend on private benevolence for meeting some portion of human and social needs will require a partnership in which government ensures equity and the availability of consistent and reliable resources, while private philanthropy provides creativity, competitiveness, independence, flexibility, and proximity.

So we come logically to the second challenge—how do we manage the process? If the first challenge is conceptual, the second is functional. In a truly benevolent community, the private and public are not mutually exclusive, but mutually reinforcing, working together dialectically to create and nurture each other. Extensive cooperation between government and the private voluntary sector has deep roots in the history of the United States and Europe, but the notion of partnership has also been at times a code word for government abandonment. An effective partnership will need to be based, therefore, on at least six basic principles or guidelines.

1. A recognition that private philanthropy serves best as an alternative to the governmental process rather than simply as an adjunct to, or a substitute for, government programs.
2. A recognition that democratic governments are consensus-driven and must promote the general welfare, while those who engage in private philanthropy are often compassion-driven, taking risks that government cannot take or the public may not want to take.
3. An understanding of the distinction between government's role in ensuring equity and excellence, and the voluntary nonprofit sector's role in providing flexibility, proximity, and creativity.
4. An agreement that each sector should do what it does best, with each gaining strength from the other rather than taking on unrealistic responsibilities.
5. A common understanding that while the resources available for private voluntary action and the resources available to government are disproportionate, the experience and perspectives of individuals from both sectors are equally critical to effective partnership.
6. An ultimate commitment to go beyond charity to create community-based wealth, using public incentives to induce or leverage private incentives.

It is this spirit of partnership that is reflected in stage IV of the evolution of the charitable impulse in which some individuals recognized the limitations of private benevolence and thus worked to create a benevolent community. For some, it led to the practice of a new form of beneficence, which made a distinction between charity and philanthropy, emphasizing the need for a collective civic commitment to the former and a more personal and private practice of the latter.

A third challenge to the benevolent community is economic—how do we mobilize the resources? Government deficits, increased economic competition across national boundaries, fluctuations in the stock markets, and a decline in the West of the share of the economy financed through the private largesse of foundations and corporate giving programs have caused public attention to turn to the economics of benevolence. Will there be a great enough economic base to support and maintain the helping traditions that have seen neighbors helping neighbors and those in the mainstream of the economy helping those on the margins?

This concern has led to a very special form of anxiety in the United States, where economic growth has come to be taken for granted and private beneficence has become an integral part of the process of meeting social needs. A new book by Yale historian Paul Kennedy argues that the United States today—like Edwardian England, Bourbon France, and Hapsburg Spain—is an empire in decline.[22] Professor Kennedy's book, *The Rise and Fall of the Great Powers,* comes on the heels of a widely circulated article by Peter G. Peterson, a former American Secretary of Commerce, who now heads a large investment firm. Published in the *Atlantic Monthly,* the article contends that America has let its infrastructure crumble, its foreign markets decline, its productivity dwindle, its savings evaporate, and its budget and borrowing burgeon. And now the day of reckoning is at hand.[23]

The economic challenge, then, is two-fold. On the supply side of benevolence, there is uncertainty about how much money is likely to be available in public revenues and private resources to meet community needs. On the demand side, there has been an explosion of social needs, running the gamut from the threat of AIDS to the predicament of an underclass whose social pathologies appear to be an intergenerational legacy.

The fourth challenge follows logically on the heels of the economic challenge. It is psychological and moral—how do we motivate future generations to commit themselves to the civic purposes and civic passion that a benevolent community requires?

We have already seen that there appears to be a direct relationship between community and philanthropy. The sentiment of generosity and of concern for neighbor is likely to increase as the sense of community evolves or expands. The reverse also appears to be true. The sentiment diminishes as the sense of community declines. This means that the prerequisite to benevolence is community. The challenge is to transform a natural affinity for primary communities into a sentiment that embraces secondary communities as well.

The answer to the question of how we motivate future generations to commit themselves to both private philanthropy and a benevolent community may lie in what we have learned about the four stages of consciousness in the evolution of the charitable impulse: 1) our children must be taught compassionate values, learning at an early age that if the strong exploit the weak, or the rich ignore the needy, the future of our society is gravely impaired; 2) compassionate values must be reinforced by intermediary institutions, parables, myths, and other forms of cultural transmission if they are to lead to active virtues like philanthropy; 3) a strong sense of the interdependence between the self and society must be cultivated; and 4) there must be awareness of both the potential and the limits of private benevolence in establishing or sustaining a caring society.

In concluding his essay "Philanthropy, Pomp and Patronage," Mordechai Feingold wrote that his purpose was "to demonstrate the necessity of scrutinizing motives in any discussion of philanthropy ... not in order to cast aspersion on the benefactors or pass moral judgement, but simply to credit human nature and the historical process with their due complexity."[24] Much the same can be said about this volume, with one exception. A deliberate attempt has been made here to trace the evolution of the philanthropic impulse from the development of an altruistic personality to the leap of consciousness that recognizes the interdependence of the private, public, and political life.

These profiles have demonstrated more clearly than most theories about altruism or charity that while human nature is complex and even contradictory, it contains a wide range of possibilities. Those who seek to encourage private generosity—or to nurture and preserve a benevolent community—can take heart from these portraits of how the caring tendencies of human nature were developed, amplified, and practiced in unlikely places and under less than encouraging circumstances. There has been no intention to identify philanthropy exclusively with the very rich, nor should it be assumed that the conclusions reached apply exclusively to benevolent wealth. Those who give out of more limited and ordinary means may be even more deserving of honor and celebration, but a primary purpose of this work has been to demonstrate and encourage an alternative tradition to the money culture of the self-indulgent wealthy, to present a mix of people, places, and times whose life stories genuinely provide a world-view of giving and culture, of personalities and motivations.

Another aim of these profiles and the accompanying essays has been to demonstrate the relationship between philanthropy and community, between giving and belonging; to show that a society's ability to cultivate a shared commitment to a common good is inextricably tied to its ability to break down the barriers that make the more narrow and exclusive "we" and "they" groups the primary centers of meaning and belonging. Kinship, friendship, neighborhoods, and nations all have legitimate claims on our loyalty and largesse, but if they are allowed to restrict rather than transform our relationship to the rest of humankind, they are likely to lead to contradictions rather than coherences, creating conflict rather than cultivating community.

While many in our time continue the effort to form a perfect union, much attention is given to the role of individualism in our history. It remains a major theme of historical analysis and self-understanding. But as Francis Fitzgerald argues in *Cities on a Hill*, there is also a less explored American tendency to start over again in groups, to build new communities. It has happened with some fair frequency that groups of Americans just stopped doing what they were doing, took themselves off, and started something new.[25]

In these periods, visionaries would appear—Joseph Smith, Susan B. Anthony, William Lloyd Garrison, Mary Baker Eddy—and in a country known for its marketplace, these visionaries would find mass followings.[26]

While few Americans seek to build totally new communities, many are nevertheless visionaries who believe that it is always possible to start over again and if necessary reinvent themselves. Rebirth and reform are quintessentially American. If a sense of community is generally a prerequisite for philanthropy and voluntarism, as it appears from this study, it may be necessary to recapture the vision of John Winthrop, the first governor of the Massachusetts Bay Colony. His vision of "a city upon a hill" had all the earmarks of the evolution of consciousness we have seen in these profiles. Once again, the challenge is to build benevolent communities in which we not only "delight in each other, but 'seek to make others' conditions our own, rejoice together, labor and suffer together, always having before our eyes our community as members of the same body."

Those who involve themselves in the social needs and problems of others will find that there is something in the nature of the relationship that is likely to transform them, compel them, and engage them with themselves and their neighbors in a brand new way. And once they discover the ability to make a difference for an AIDS patient, to change the life of a child who has become accustomed to going to bed hungry, or to salvage an endangered cultural institution, the charitable impulse, which starts out as a very personal and solitary drive, is likely to be transformed into a larger commitment to developing or maintaining a caring society.

The *Nouveau Riche* as Moneygivers

16

Philanthropy and the New Concentrations of Wealth

WHAT CAN WE EXPECT in the future? Will the newly rich outside the United States be moneygivers or simply generators and consumers of wealth? Are there communities and cultures that are more likely to inculcate the other-serving values that lead to private philanthropy? A brief review of examples from diverse cultures provides reason for both optimism and caution.

ASIA

It is widely assumed that the rise of Japan as an economic superpower has produced a new class of super-rich. But the government that has encouraged and strongly supported the development of highly successful transnational business enterprises has not been as supportive of the accumulation of individual wealth. A tax policy with an 80 percent top bracket for individuals, and inheritance taxes up to 75 percent of an estate, has kept Japan from joining those developed societies with a disproportionate concentration of wealth at the top. Moreover, the Japanese emphasis is on the responsibility of the group for the well-being of its members rather than on the benevolence of the individual.

Even under very restrictive tax laws, industrialists like Knonsuke Matsushita, the founder of a consumer electronics company and the largest taxpayer in Japan, and Shoyi Uehara, chairman of Taisho

Pharmaceutical, have managed to propel themselves into the orbit of the world's wealthiest. But they contribute to the well-being of their community primarily through the business enterprises they control, rather than simply through the private assets they own outright. Even men like Ryoichi Sasakawa who advocate and practice private philanthropy tend to do most of their good works through their businesses.

Thus, while the cultural traditions of Japan do not stress private benevolence, a new public philosophy is emerging that sees corporate philanthropy as an integral part of Japanese society. Not only are the top private corporations taking on an increasingly visible role in dealing with domestic social needs, but the penetration of Japanese business enterprises into other cultures is expanding the notion of corporate responsibility to include non-Japanese communities as well.

Like the early Benefaction Society, the Kannon Ko, established in 1829, the modern Japanese business corporation is the most significant aggregation of private assets through which the charitable impulse is expressed in Japan. But this could soon change. The Japanese parliament is under heavy pressure to overhaul the nation's tax laws. Former prime minister Noboru Takeshita and his ruling Liberal Democratic Party are committed to shifting the tax burden by lowering income tax rates and imposing a sales tax. Such a change would undoubtedly lead to larger concentrations of private wealth in the hands of individuals, creating the opportunity for new forms of voluntary assistance and private philanthropy.

Asian wealth outside Japan is also spreading, with much of it in the hands of the overseas Chinese, who are generally regarded as the most frugal of the world's rich, generous in philanthropy while spending very little on themselves. One of the most prominent is Y. C. Wang, the founder and chairman of the Formosa Plastics Group. It is reported that while he gave $250 million to a private hospital, he was upset when his staff spent $1,000 on a new carpet. The manifestations of new Asian wealth can also be seen in Seoul, Taipei, and Singapore, but it is the Japanese who are likely to have the most influence on private giving in the future. With the GNP of Japan now second only to the United States and the country facing increasing demands to "share the burden" of international social responsibilities, government and business leaders have responded with a commitment to a significant increase in foreign assistance, both government aid and private philanthropy.

EUROPE

While many are convinced that we are seeing the dawn of an Asian century, others harbor visions of the return of a powerful Europe, hoping that the more tightly integrated European Community scheduled to come into being in 1992 will mean new wealth and influence. This Eurocentric view of the future is increasingly affirmed by those who believe that what lies ahead is what we have already experienced. For them, greatness lies in a return to the purity of the past rather than in the acceptance of the pluralism of the future. While the social transformations now taking place argue for a different conclusion, it would be a mistake to conclude, however, that the decline of European dominance means the disappearance of European influence and wealth.

The more the concentration of private wealth changes, the more it looks the same. The richest families are still those of royalty. Any look at private wealth in Europe must thus begin with Queen Elizabeth II of the United Kingdom and Queen Beatrix of the Netherlands. Both are billionaires whose wealth is tax-free. The poet laureate Ted Hughes once described Queen Elizabeth as a mirror reflecting what the English like to think they are, regal and cultured, continuing a tradition of *noblesse oblige*. But there are still those whose use of wealth reflects social and moral imperatives that go beyond the obligations of nobility. Like the working classes who responded to the spiritual appeal of John Wesley and the social sympathies of an earlier evangelicalism, there are men and women of means who continue to believe that self-sacrifice and other-serving values are essential to liberty and social order.

The Victorian confidence that the charity of the rich could cope with poverty and other social pathologies has lost its hold on the English mind, but the increasingly popular notion of a "welfare-pluralism" suggests a continued dependency on benevolent wealth.

Italy has an old money set that goes to great pains to hide personal wealth. Some observers say it is the dominance of the Catholic tradition that has made some people feel guilty about accumulating wealth, while others attribute the preference for anonymity to a desire to keep private assets out of view of tax collectors and the kidnappers who terrorize the rich. Yet, it is generally known that the Agnelli family, of Fiat fame, rank among the world's wealthiest, while the Benetton family, who have almost as many clothing stores as McDonalds has fast-food restaurants, are quickly moving up the ladder. The legacy of Adriano Olivetti still serves as a model of benevolent wealth through the foundation run by members of his family. Named after the great industrialist and man of broad cultural and political interests, the Fondazione Adriano Olivetti is highly regarded for its contributions to the debate on the problems of democracy in Italy. There is no indication, however, that the newly rich are ready to walk in Olivetti's footsteps.

The French, on the other hand, have done an even better job than the Japanese in keeping a lid on the accumulation of private wealth. The national disdain for the passions of the old money culture is reflected in high taxes and state control of industry. However, a vocal minority regularly expresses opposition to the tax rates, social change, and the burdens created by immigrants, especially North Africans. And not surprisingly, it is the immigrant issue more than any other that casts a dark shadow on France's image of itself as a benevolent community. Independent, nationalistic, and self-conscious, the French are generally regarded as the most self-assured people in Europe, but their individualism is tempered by a tendency to turn to government when they are in personal distress or when their neighbor is in need. It is sometimes said that when anything goes wrong, even the weather, there is a tendency to blame the state and to look to it for compensation.

The late President Charles de Gaulle's greatest fear was that nationalism might diminish and his countrymen become bickering tribes. Constantly warning of the need for social cohesion, he once asked in jest, "How can you govern a country that makes 365 kinds of cheese?" The sense of being special, even superior, continues to make for a strong national identity. The French know who they are and like what they see, but it is precisely this love of themselves that makes it difficult for some Frenchmen to open up their society to immigrants who are different. While the intellectuals and their allies on the left of the political spectrum continue to call for a more open and compassionate society, this is not likely to alter the uses of private wealth. The *nouveau riche* are placing emphasis on private enterprise and limited government, but when it comes to meeting social needs, they tend to adhere to the old paradigms that emphasize the social role of government rather than the development of a nonprofit, voluntary sector.

The Scandinavians, the people of Northern Europe, are especially known for their generosity and their ideas about fairness and social obligation. While there are certainly differences among the many nations of the region, they have organized their societies similarly, preferring egalitarian-minded welfare states rather than depending in any way on the benevolence of private wealth. For many in Europe and elsewhere, these countries have become models of what it means to live in a competitive, interdependent world without being either master or subject. The Carlsberg Foundation in Denmark is a very important philanthropic legacy, but it represents the old wealth be-qeathed by the Jacobsen family, who established the Carlsberg Brewery in the late Nineteenth Century. Likewise in Sweden, the dominant expression of private benevolence is not the *nouveau riche*, but the Bank of Sweden Tercentenary Foundation, which was established in 1968 as part of the observance of the tricentennial of the oldest central bank in the world.

The Dutch also have a tax-heavy welfare state, but there is at the same time a surprising concentration of private wealth. Like the Italians, the rich in the Netherlands jealously guard their privacy, but they tend to be a little more creative, often using family foundations to hold their assets and control their companies. Jos von Hezewijk, a scholar who published the book *The Top Elite of the Netherlands*, claims that the wealthy Dutch would rather talk about their sex lives than their money, although their sex lives are far less interesting.

Two major exceptions are the Bernard van Leer Foundation and the Prins Bernhard Fonds. The van Leer Foundation was created in 1949 by Bernard van Leer, who in his will bequeathed the entire share of capital of the Van Leer Group of Companies to the foundation after his death in 1958. While its headquarters are in the Hague, the foundation supports programs in more than thirty countries, including the United States. The Prins Bernhard Fonds, located in Amsterdam, has brought a novel twist to private benevolence. Its original endowment was established in 1940 for the purpose of buying military hardware for the British and Dutch governments, but the fund, which now funds cultural properties, now shares in the revenues of the Dutch lottery.

Wealth in Germany was interrupted by fascism and defeat in two World Wars, yet several family dynasties managed to survive. One of the most successful was the von Finch family, whose members made their fortune in banking. Upon his death in 1980, August von Finch left his sons an estate worth over $1 billion. Both the Fritz Thyssen Stiftung and the Robert Bosch Stiftung embody old wealth that managed to survive war and economic collapse to later emerge as large private foundations. The Stiftung Volkswagenwerk, on the other hand, owes its existence to an agreement between the Federal Republic of Germany and the State of Lower Saxony bringing to an end a controversy concerning ownership of the huge Volkswagen enterprise after 1945.

The postwar boom in Germany, the so-called economic miracle of the 1950s and early 1960s, produced new wealth, but with high inheritance taxes. Preserving it through generations continues to be a difficult task. The oil shocks of the 1970s caused new problems as they eroded private wealth and tested the nation's commitment to those who were the victims of a declining economy. For native Germans, the economic decline was cushioned by extensive public welfare provisions, but the many immigrants in their midst posed a special problem of conscience. The question of what constitutes a benevolent community came to be asked in the context of national duty and national identity. The ambivalence about national consciousness gave way to a new German self-awareness as a large number of Germans came to believe that there were too many foreigners in the country.

Thus, benevolent wealth in Germany remains a restrictive concept. The charitable impulse is highly visible in a growing charitable sector, but like their neighbors in most of Europe, many Germans share an ambivalence about whether the individual commitment to a larger community extends to those outside the primary community. Like their neighbors, they also tend to look to the state rather than to private generosity to meet basic human needs.

It is commonplace to locate the roots of modern philanthropy on European soil while placing the potential for future growth in Asia. But what are we to make of Latin America, the Middle East, and Africa?

LATIN AMERICA

Stereotypes of wealth in Latin America abound, but not all private assets have been stashed out of the region or consumed in lavish living, as is often assumed. While wealthy South Americans are known more for their self-indulgent life styles than for their contribution to the welfare of their neighbors, it was the social conscience and commitment to national development that led Sebastiano Ferraz de Carmargo to help build the Trans-Amazon Highway and the world's largest hydro-electric dam in his native Brazil. With a fortune of more than one billion dollars, he combines the entrepreneurial impulse with a sense of civic duty and social obligation. Like Eugenio Mendoza in Venezeula, Amalita Fortabut in Argentina, and others in Latin America who are less well known, Carmargo epitomizes the spirit of the nationalist who uses his private resources for nation-building.

Much of the private wealth in Latin America is now mortgaged to the outside banks and other lenders who have made most of the countries south of the American border huge debtor nations. Thus, the future of private philanthropy in this region is likely to be influenced more by the spirit of benevolence of individuals and families of relatively modest means than by large aggregations of wealth. The decision by President Oscar Arias of Costa Rica to use his Nobel Peace Prize money to start a foundation reflects the potential for cooperative approaches that bring together multiple private endowments under one umbrella.

AFRICA

On the African continent, wealth is primarily in the hands of expatriates and men and women of European heritage whose families gained advantage through formal or informal policies of separate development. Most have used their wealth to sustain luxurious life-styles or to prop up the political and economic systems that have provided them advantages; but a few, like Harry Oppenheimer in South Africa, have been major philanthropists.

It is not unusual to hear researchers and scholars lament the absence of a philanthropic tradition in Africa. Their views are often clouded by the physical distance from the African continent or the psychological distance from African culture. But they also reflect a common failure to recognize the close relationship in Africa between the practice of philanthropy and the boundaries of community. The overwhelming commitment to the family, village, or tribe has made it difficult for larger communal groups to command African loyalty and largesse. As Jennifer Seymour Whitaker points out in *How Can Africa Survive,* when Africans go to the city they don't so much leave their village as they take it with them. No matter how high they rise politically or how successful they become economically, they are likely to spend much of their time, on and off the job, boosting the fortunes of their primary communal group. Their sense of the common good rarely extends to the boundaries of artificially created nation-states.

In Africa, neither the flirtation with new wealth during the oil boom nor the participation in an international economy appears to have changed traditional African loyalties or expanded traditional boundaries of social obligation and moral duty. While the influence of Christianity on values and attitudes can be seen and felt, the influence of Islam is even stronger in many areas. Both continue to compete with traditional religion and culture for the African mind. There is very little wealth in Africa, and the prospects for the future remain limited. Thus, it is correct to note the absence of the philanthropic vehicles used by the benevolent rich, but it is a mistake to assume the absence of a benevolent tradition. The idea of *homo-communalis,* man's existence in community and his obligations to others, is as much a part of African metaphysics as it was a part of early Greek culture.

MIDDLE EAST

Probably the most stereotyped of the newly rich are the Arabs. Stories about wealthy sheiks in Las Vegas and wealthy students in Cambridge and elsewhere have been printed by journalists fascinated with the absurd and reported by television commentators intrigued by the mysterious. Very little is known about men like Osmon Ahmed Osman in Egypt, who is worth an estimated $1.5 billion and was close to the late President Anwar Sadat. His benefactions have helped to erect hospitals, houses, and even bridges.

As in Europe, the largest concentrations of wealth in the Middle East are in the hands of royalty. Leading the list is King Fahd of Saudi Arabia; there is no real separation between the nation's treasury and his private fortune. Running a close second to King Fahd is a fellow monarch, Zaid al Nahayan of Abu Dhabi. Both are known for spending freely and, sometimes, generously, but King Fahd has taken an additional step into organized philanthropy as head of the King Faisal Foundation, named in honor of his father. The initial fund of the foundation was contributed by the heirs of the late King Faisal from his estate, but members of the family have also made individual contributions. The foundation uses these funds on various educational, scientific, and charitable activities that benefit Muslims and enhance their progress and advancement inside and outside the Kingdom of Saudi Arabia.

The idea of philanthropy is at the heart of Arab culture. Its roots lie in both the requirements of Islam and the early bedouin ethics of the desert. But as long as the nations of the Middle East feel the necessity to turn inward exclusively for the sense of belonging that provides meaning, dignity, and self-esteem, the charitable impulse is likely to continue to be directed toward the members of the primary community rather than a universal humanity.

THE SOVIET UNION

Can the civic values of Rousseau, Locke, and de Tocqueville find a home in a society dominated by the legacy of Marx and Lenin? Until recently, many Sovietologists would have dismissed the thought as the musings of the naive. Yet everywhere one turns in the Soviet Union, private citizens are forming voluntary organizations and developing charitable alternatives to the governmental process.

Much has been written about "glastnost" and "perestroika," the twin towers of openness and restructuring. But this is only one side of the story. The real story may be the emergence of a charitable sector, the flourishing of private initiatives, and the formation of foundations and other forms of organized philanthropy. The recently formed foundations are unique to their cultural and economic context. They are fueled by the small contributions of many Soviet citizens rather than the benevolent wealth of a few.

There are local foundations like the Lithuanian Women's Charitable Fund in Vilnius; funds for historic preservation in Kiev; and funds for environmental advocacy in Leningrad. There are regional funds supporting the aspirations of ethnic groups in the Baltic states and there are national and international foundations headquartered in Moscow. All of these are new foundations at an early stage of development. Many make no distinction between charity—healing the sick and caring for the isolated elderly—and philanthropy—calculated giving that seeks to eliminate causes rather than simply ameliorate consequences. Others mix charitable intent with political action. In the absence of a regulatory framework or a grantmaking culture, government authorities are simply tolerating, for the moment, many activities that were formerly underground.

Where is the money to come from to keep all these new funds going? What social needs are to be met through private benevolence? While neither workers nor pensioners make very much money, there is even less opportunity to spend it effectively. Housing is poor by any standard, but it is inexpensive; families are crowded into small flats, but they have a roof above their heads and beds on which to sleep. Education and health services are free, the basic foods inexpensive, and consumer goods cheap in quality and in cost. Thus, citizens with bank accounts of unspendable rubles are contributing their unused funds to meet social needs that have been, until recently, denied or hidden from public view.

A 1989 delegation to the Soviet Union from the American-based Council on Foundations heard tragic tales of homelessness in rural areas, of the isolated elderly and handicapped, of orphaned and neglected children, of extreme environmental abuse and, even worse, stories of human lives where hope and dignity no longer reside. Even the newspapers and television commentators now report openly on unmet social needs and unsolved social problems. Private funds are being used to rewrite the distorted history of the Stalin era, to restore buildings and gravesites, to rehabilitate Afghan veterans, and to reclaim broken lives and broken limbs.

When queried about the source of the charitable impulse, why so many people are donating money for charitable activities, a Moscow ecclesiastic described Soviet society as an essentially religious society that maintained fundamentally religious values even in the days when sentiments like charity were suspect. The new charitable sector may thus be a monument to the resilience of the human spirit. But it is also, for the moment at least, a series of contradictions.

There is creativity in search of institutional expression—people excited by the possibility of addressing, directly, social needs and social aspirations that have been ignored or stifled for seventy-five years. There is an almost metaphysical search for a common moral code, a turning to the church and other forms of spiritual outlets that have been discouraged or denied. There is a renaissance of culture and a new freedom of the mind, a willingness to criticize the past publicly, to think new thoughts and to dream new dreams.

But in the midst of the incredible spiritual, intellectual, and political ferment supported by the new philanthropy, there is a limited knowledge of process; questions about how to maximize the impact of the charitable dollar are just beginning to be raised. There is uncertainty about whether the new charitable sector will really make a difference. There is also anxiety about whether the new openness will last, a lingering fear that the conservative bureaucrats and other

agents of the state will not permit this new freedom to continue.
Yet, any objective observer must conclude that the new spirit flooding
the charitable marketplace will be difficult to contain. It has both
the moral force of shared community values and the momentum
of a people who are determined to express publicly the compassion
and generosity that have so long been lying just below the surface.

These, then, are some of the people and passions that are shaping
the future of wealth and social conscience outside the United States.
While many of the private benefactions of the *nouveau riche* stem
from motives that are altruistic and noble, others reflect the same
mix of self-interest and public benefit that led the American president
John F. Kennedy to suggest in his 1963 inaugural address that, "If
a free society cannot help the many who are poor, it cannot save
the few who are rich."

Three ideas are converging to create optimism about the future
of private philanthropy in a pluralistic social fabric. The first is the
idea of a civil society, the notion that society is distinct from government
and that government is but one of several sectors with civic responsibilities. In many parts of the world, the initiative for social change
and civic improvement is shifting to voluntary groups that operate
outside of direct state control. While the leaders of these groups have
no intention of relieving government of its legitimate social responsibilities, they are appealing to private individuals and institutions
to play a larger social role.

The second is the idea that the individual belongs to a large community of strangers as well as a local network of friends and, therefore, has opportunities and responsibilities that transcend the traditional centers of meaning and belonging. The increasing interdependence of the world economy and the revolution in communications have made possible such a high degree of networking that
people who formerly viewed their responsibilities as primarily to themselves and their families are taking on the mentality of citizens of
a world community. This is especially true among the wealthy where

people with common interests are readily locating one another across national and cultural boundaries and entering into communication about social needs as well as social aspirations. Moreover, the new information technologies are constantly bombarding formerly isolated enclaves of wealth with visual images of the poor and others in need. And because they are no longer invisible, the poor are difficult to ignore or dismiss.

The third is the idea that people coming together in a nongovernmental context, away from the pressures of state policy and state politics, can effectively change social realities. Even in those societies where there are no large concentrations of private wealth, we are seeing the encouragement of voluntary action and the mobilization of private resources for civic improvement. Until recently, it was virtually unthinkable, for example, that Soviet citizens concerned about the preservation of a historic building or the pollution of a river would come together to form private foundations or to take private action as they are now doing.

It is thus increasingly important that those who seek to maintain a caring society, who believe in the value of private philanthropy both to those who give and those who receive, not only applaud, but actively promote the sense of interconnectedness and belonging that leads to civic idealism and behavioral altruism. At its best, benevolent wealth can function as a counterbalance to dominant social interests, as a champion of the underserved and the underprivileged, and as an alternative to the governmental process. In an interdependent world, private philanthropy can rise above nationalism to investigate global solutions to international issues. It can borrow and transplant the best from cultural and scientific establishments to societies in desperate need. Miracle drugs, green revolution grains, and human rights networks are all international achievements that owe part of their success to private philanthropy.

Hopefully, recent celebrations of wealth by the wealthy, and those who want to be wealthy, was a passing phase and we are ready to replace consumption with caring, selfishness with service. If it is true—as some observers contend—that belief in a common good is back in fashion, the *nouveau riche* no longer need the illusions of a money culture to provide meaning and belonging. Money can be a means toward an end again and not an end to be pursued for its own sake. If the old civic values and moral traditions are indeed ascendant, there is reason for optimism that private philanthropy will continue to be an essential vehicle for doing good in the world, a venue for promoting as well as practicing virtue, for shaping as well as salvaging community.

All of society—rich and poor—can thus gain confidence from the ultimate potential of private engagement captured by Robert Kennedy's statement at the University of Cape Town in South Africa in 1966: "Each time a man (or woman) stands up for an ideal or acts to improve the lot of others, he sends forth a tiny ripple of hope, and crossing each other from a million different centers of energy and daring, these ripples build a current that can sweep down the mightiest wall of resistance."

NOTES

PROLOGUE

1. I am indebted to Dr. Samuel Oliner, a professor at Humboldt State University in California, for sharing with me the early conclusions of his work.
2. Marcel Mauss, *The Gift* (New York and London: Norton and Company, 1967).
3. See the arguments of Robert Bellah and associates in *Habits of the Heart* (Berkeley and London: University of California Press, 1986).
4. Parker Palmer, *The Company of Strangers* (New York: The Crossroad Publishing Company, 1981).
5. Bellah, op. cit.
6. Joel T. Rosenthal, *The Purchase of Paradise* (London and Toronto: Routledge and Kegan Paul, 1972), p. 8.
7. Ibid., p. 8.
8. Jacob Neusner, *Foundation News*, vol. 25, no. 5 (Washington, D.C.: Council on Foundations, 1985), p. 41.
9. Reinhold Niebuhr, *Man's Nature and His Communities* (New York: Charles Scribner's Sons, 1965), p. 85.

PART I. WEALTH AND CIVIC DUTY

1. W. K. Jordan, *Philanthropy in England*, 1480–1660 (New York: Russell Sage Foundation, 1959), p. 143.
2. Kathleen McCarthy, *Noblesse Oblige* (Chicago: University of Chicago Press, 1982), p. 3.

3. Ronald W. Clark, *A Biography of the Nuffield Foundation* (London: Longman Group Ltd., 1972), p. 6.
4. Ibid., p. 1.
5. Ibid., p. 3.
6. Ibid., p. 11.
7. Ibid., p. 11.
8. R. J. Overy, *William Morris, Viscount Nuffield* (London: Europa Publications, Ltd., 1950), p. 102.
9. P. W. Andrews and E. Brunner, *The Life of Lord Nuffield* (Oxford, B. Blackwell, 1955), p. 42.
10. Overy, op. cit., p. 101.
11. Andrews and Brunner, op. cit., p. 4.
12. Overy, op. cit., p. 4.
13. Ibid., p. 105.
14. Andrews and Brunner, op. cit., p. 4.
15. Overy, op. cit., p. 106.
16. Sir Miles Thomas, *Out on the Wing* (London: M. Joseph, 1964), p. 130.
17. Overy, op. cit. pp. 108–109.
18. *Economist*, CXIX (London: 1934), p. 834.
19. *Motor Trader*, CLXXV (London: 1949), p. 44.
20. Overy, op. cit., p. 114.
21. Clark, op. cit., p. 5.
22. See "The Oppenheimer Phenomenon" in *The South African Connection* by Ruth First, Jonathan Steele, and Christabel Gurney (London: Temple Smith, 1972).
23. Ibid., p. 204.
24. Ibid., p. 208.
25. *Mission to South Africa: The Commonwealth Report* (New York: Penguin Books, 1986), p. 44.
26. Ibid., p. 45.

PART II. THE RELIGIOUS IMPERATIVE

1. Edna Healey, *Lady Unknown: The Life of Angela Burdett-Coutts* (London: Sidgwick and Jackson, 1978), p. 222.
2. Ibid., p. 222.

3. David Owen gives a fuller account of the relationship between Charles Dickens and Angela Burdett-Coutts in *English Philanthropy* (Cambridge: Harvard University Press, 1964).
4. Clara Burdett Patterson, *Angela Burdett-Coutts and the Victorians* (London, 1953).
5. Edgar Johnson, *Letters from Charles Dickens to Angela Burdett-Coutts* (London: 1953).
6. Ibid., pp. 77–82.
7. Healey, op. cit., p. 89.
8. Ibid., p. 91.
9. *Reader's Digest* (April 1963), pp. 248–249.
10. Ibid., p. 250.
11. Berem Sh. Saklatvda and K. Khosla, *Jamsetji Tata* (Publications Division, Government of India, 1970), p. 3.
12. *Foundation News* (November–December, 1978), p. 250.
13. Elwin Verrier, *The Story of Tata Steel* (Bombay: Commercial Printing Press Private Limited, 1958), p. 14.
14. Ibid., p. 131.
15. *Asiatic Review*, XLIV (no. 159) (London: 1948).
16. D. E. Wacha, *The Life and Work of J. N. Tata* (Madras: Ganesh and Company Publishers, 1915), p. 46.
17. Ibid., p. 47.
18. Wacha, op. cit., p. 111.
19. Saklatvda and Khosla, op. cit., p. 56.
20. Ibid., p. 57.
21. Saklatvda and Khosla, op. cit., p. 12.
22. *Foundation News*, op. cit., p. 252.
23. Anne Vernon, *A Quaker Businessman* (York, England: William Sessions Limited, 1982), p. 10.
24. George Malcolm Young, *Victorian England* (London: Oxford University Press, 1960).
25. Vernon, op. cit., p. 22.
26. Ibid., p. 42.
27. Ibid., p. 62.
28. See his essay, "Pauperism in England and Wales," in the files of the Rowntree Trust.
29. Vernon, op. cit., p. 99.
30. Ibid., p. 152.

PART III. THE QUEST FOR MEANING

1. For a fuller discussion of this thesis, see *The Feast of Fools* by Harvey Cox (Cambridge: Harvard University Press, 1969).
2. Lewis Mumford, *The Myth of the Machine* (New York: Harcourt, Brace, 1967).
3. Albert Camus, *The Rebel* (New York: Knopf, 1956), p. 296.
4. Ralph Hewins, *Mr. Five Per Cent, The Story of Calouste Gulbenkian* (New York: Rinehart, 1958).
5. *The Washington Post*, "The Forgotten Survivors," Saturday, April 27, 1985.
6. Hewins, op. cit., p. viii.
7. Ibid., p. 253.
8. Ibid., p. 208.
9. *Polly van Leer: Reflections on Her Thoughts* (Jerusalem, Israel: The van Leer Jerusalem Foundation, 1974), p. 53.
10. Ibid., p. 7.
11. Ibid., p. 7.

PART IV. MIXED MOTIVES, OR TAINTED GENEROSITY

1. *The Eagle*, 61 (No. 13) Dec. 8, 1986, p. 7.
2. Ibid., p. 7.
3. While Khashoggi's activities have been widely covered by the press for more than a decade, the most definitive information on his life is to be found in *The Richest Man in the World* by Ronald Kessler (New York: Warner Books, Inc., 1986).
4. Ibid., p. 7.

PART V. THE BENEVOLENT COMMUNITY

1. Warren Weaver, *U.S. Philanthropic Foundations* (New York: Harper and Row, 1967).
2. Joseph C. Goulden, *The Money Givers* (New York: Random House, 1971).
3. Teresa Odendahl, ed., *America's Wealthy and the Future of Foundations* (New York: The Foundation Center, 1987).
4. Ronald W. Clark, *A Biography of the Nuffield Foundation* (London: Longman Group Ltd., 1972).

5. J. Irwin Miller, "Time to Listen," *Foundation News* (May/June 1984), p. 17.

6. Michael Schulman and Eva Mekler, *Bringing Up a Moral Child* (Reading, MA: Addison-Wesley, 1985).

7. "Great Altruists," *New York Times*, March 5, 1985.

8. See Robert Reich, *Tales of a New America* (New York: Times Books, 1987).

9. Ibid., p. 7.

10. H. Richard Niebuhr, *Christ and Culture* (New York: Harper and Row, 1951).

11. For an excellent formation of this thesis, see Reich, op. cit., p. 9.

12. Edwin O. Reischaeur, *The Japanese* (Tokyo: Charles E. Tuttle Company, 1977), p. 127.

13. "An Open Letter: The Public and Its Education" (Philadelphia: Board of Christian Education, United Presbyterian Church, U.S.A., 1969), p. 14.

14. M. Scott Peck, *The Different Drum* (New York: Simon and Schuster, 1987), p. 77.

15. Ibid., pp. 83–84.

16. Marion Fremont-Smith, *Foundations and Government* (New York: Russell Sage, 1965).

17. James Douglas, *Why Charity?* (Beverly Hills and London: Sage Publications, 1983), p. 15.

18. *Report of the Nathan Commission on the Laws and Practices Relating to Charitable Trust*, British Government, 1952, para. 44.

19. David Owen, *English Philanthropy* (Cambridge: Harvard University Press, 1964), p. 6.

20. Lester Salaman, *Of Market Failure, Voluntary Failure, and Third Party Government* (Washington, D.C.: The Urban Institute, 1987).

21. Frank Prochaska, *The Voluntary Impulse* (London: Faber and Faber Ltd., 1988), p. 4.

22. Paul M. Kennedy, *The Rise and Fall of the Great Powers: Economic Change and Military Conflict from 1500 to 2000* (New York: Random House, 1987).

23. Peter G. Peterson, "The Morning After," *The Atlantic Monthly*, October 1987.

24. Mordechai Feingold, "Philanthropy, Pomp and Patronage," *Daedalus* (Cambridge, MA: Winter 1987), p. 177.

25. Frances Fitzgerald, *Cities on a Hill* (New York: Simon and Schuster, 1986), p. 23.
26. Ibid., p. 24.

INDEX